Cambridge L

Elements in Early Chris
edited by
Garrick V. Allen
University of Glasgow

MAXIMOS THE CONFESSOR

Androprimacy and Sexual Difference

Luis Josué Salés
Scripps College

CAMBRIDGE
UNIVERSITY PRESS

CAMBRIDGE
UNIVERSITY PRESS

Shaftesbury Road, Cambridge CB2 8EA, United Kingdom

One Liberty Plaza, 20th Floor, New York, NY 10006, USA

477 Williamstown Road, Port Melbourne, VIC 3207, Australia

314–321, 3rd Floor, Plot 3, Splendor Forum, Jasola District Centre,
New Delhi – 110025, India

103 Penang Road, #05–06/07, Visioncrest Commercial, Singapore 238467

Cambridge University Press is part of Cambridge University Press & Assessment,
a department of the University of Cambridge.

We share the University's mission to contribute to society through the pursuit of
education, learning and research at the highest international levels of excellence.

www.cambridge.org
Information on this title: www.cambridge.org/9781009492195
DOI: 10.1017/9781009492188

First published 2025

A catalogue record for this publication is available from the British Library.

ISBN 978-1-009-49219-5 Hardback
ISBN 978-1-009-49221-8 Paperback
ISSN 2977-0327 (online)
ISSN 2977-0319 (print)

Maximos the Confessor

Androprimacy and Sexual Difference

Elements in Early Christian Literature

DOI: 10.1017/ 9781009492188
First published online: February 2025

Luis Josué Salés
Scripps College
Author for correspondence: Luis Josué Salés, lsales@scrippscollege.edu

Abstract: Maximos affirms in various texts (such as Difficulty 41) that sexual differentiation into male and female is inconsistent with the divine intention and will therefore be eschatologically eradicated. His affirmations have elicited a half-dozen conflicting interpretations, such as the metaphorization of these statements, where "male" refers to drive (*thymos*) and "female" to desire (*epithymia*), which become subordinate to reason (*logos*). Others maintain that he refers to the resolution of male–female agonistics. Yet others have criticized accounts that mollify the starkness of Maximos' affirmations. This Element goes further in arguing that Maximos tacitly envisions the elimination of sexual difference as sublimation of all sexual difference into male singularity. This Element overviews the exegetical and medical-anthropological precedents that framed Maximos thinking on this subject and examines some of his key texts, including his famed Difficulty 41 and several passages centered on explicating Eve and Adam, and Mary and Christ.

Keywords: Maximos, gender, sexual difference, androprimacy, eschatology

ISBNs: 9781009492195 (HB), 9781009492218 (PB), 9781009492188 (OC)
ISSNs: 2977-0327 (online), 2977-0319 (print)

Contents

Introduction

Maximos the Confessor (580–662) was a monk of the Roman Empire who lived through some of its most cataclysmic and defining decades.[1] He was born fifteen years after Justinian's rule (527–565), during which imperial borders were unsustainably expanded at an incalculable demographic and fiscal cost that rapidly jeopardized the state's viability. The monastic intellectual witnessed, often first-hand, the political, military, and religious conflicts that repeatedly destabilized the Empire, such as the enormously destructive Roman-Sasanian War (602–626), the Arab conquests that followed a few years later, and several Christological controversies. Against this backdrop, even the general outline of Maximos' early life has become speculative. There are three hypotheses about his provenance – Constantinople, Palestine, Alexandria – none without problems.[2] Wherever Maximos hailed from, he received an outstanding education in scriptural and Patristic exegesis and in late Platonic philosophy, which by this time was an eclectic undertaking encompassing not only the Platonic-Aristotelian corpus (then considered one philosophical system) but also certain reanimated features of Stoicism, Pythagoreanism, and other classical schools. These intellectual currents are all apparent in Maximos' oeuvre, which almost entirely consists of his ad hoc responses to petitions by acquaintances to offer his commentary on disputed texts and traditions. The shape of the Confessor's corpus is hardly surprising, as he was well connected across the Mediterranean world, especially throughout the monastic and aristocratic networks of Roman-occupied Africa from Alexandria to Carthage, and was, therefore, often called upon as a religious authority to weigh in on heady subjects. Maximos' prominence translated to a perilous conspicuousness when renewed Christological disputes became lethally political in the later decades of his life. Maximos' unflinching opposition to the court's official position, known as Monothelitism, eventually resulted in the mutilation of his right hand and tongue, the instruments through which he had theologically defied the Constantinopolitan seat of power.[3] Thus punished, but not martyred, the adamantine monk earned the honorific "the Confessor" and was exiled alongside his lifelong ascetic partner, Anastasios, to a military prison near the Black Sea in today's Georgia. He died there soon after from the torturous ordeal he endured in his crepuscular years.

Based on bibliographic entries (ca. 3,000), the Maximian corpus is currently the most studied premodern Greek Christian body of texts outside the New Testament.

---

[1] A few orienting studies: Shoemaker, *Death of a Prophet*; Penn, *Envisioning Islam*; Booth, *Crisis of Empire*; Kaldellis, *New Roman Empire*, 320–404.

[2] For an overview, see Salés, "The Other Life of Maximos the Confessor," 407–439. For a critique of Salés, see Ohme, *Kirche in der Krise*, 637–638.

[3] The belief that Christ has one divine will, rather than a human will and a divine will.

His corpus is not particularly large: Two average volumes of Migne's *Patrologia Graeca* contain nearly all his works, most of which have more recently received critical editions. Nearly all of these texts are outwardly epistolary, in the sense that they are letters in response to earlier communications, but their "inner genre," so to speak, differs considerably and includes the questions-and-answers (*erotapokriseis*) genre, common among monastics seeking wisdom from an elder through a back-and-forth series of questions and answers, the chapters (*kephalaia*) genre, a form popularized by Evagrios of Pontos to ease monastic memorization of pithy aphorisms, the scriptural and Patristic exegetical genre, and so on. These distinctions are in some sense artificial, as several of Maximos' works include features of multiple genres. For example, the *Difficulties* (aka *Ambigua*) is a very long (ca. 80,000 words) exegetical epistle seemingly in the form of an *erotapokriseis* that also relies heavily on late Platonic and Patristic commentary conventions. Thus, Maximos' work is highly varied in subjects and approaches.

Maximos was one of the last major late ancient Christian theologians and bridged the way to the early medieval Roman era. The monastic author attempted to distill some six centuries of Greek Christian thought into a system given coherence by his own idiosyncratic genius. This system is rigorous and highly technical, with the result that it often presents to first-time readers (and seasoned alike!) as a steeply sloped ascent to elusive terraces of sublime fruits that, even when found, require protracted harvesting and intellectual mastication before their nourishment becomes digestible. Nonetheless, most who have undertaken this venture affirm the worthwhileness of the trek, even if getting routinely lost or chipping a tooth on a proverbial small, hard seed appears to be an occupational hazard of the venture. It bears pondering, then, what about Maximos' thought has seemed perennially appealing to modern and postmodern scholars.

The monastic intellectual's prominence may be partly attributed to the resonance his preoccupations have found with modern audiences, including profound reflections on psychology, ethics, cosmology, spirituality, and sexual difference. Conversely, Maximos' thought is enthralling for its aspiration to an organic and intricately interwoven coherence of diverse subjects that discourages the examination of any particular one in isolation, much as the heart's function cannot be understood without also that of the brain, lungs, arteries, and veins.[4] So, while the central topic of this Element is the monastic author's view of sexual difference, it is inadvisable to treat this content without also engaging with his protology, eschatology, cosmology, anthropology, and Christology, to

---

[4] Maximos Constas has made a different point to a similar effect. See *On Difficulties in the Church Fathers* vol. 1, xxiv.

name the most salient. This much is clear in the most important text in this study, *Difficulty* 41, which lays out a fivefold division of the universe, ranging from uncreated and created at the most general level down to male and female at the most specific. Accordingly, a critical reexamination of Maximos' thought on sexual difference might carry implications beyond human corporeality alone, tracing its ripple effects across the cosmic structure that circumscribes it.

Specifically, this study is concerned with Maximos' effort to postulate an eschatological human universality that converges around an ostensibly unsexed "human" (ἄνθρωπος). In other words, in the life hereafter, sexual difference will vanish, though Maximos never spelled out the specifics of what that entailed, even if he does drop a few hints. According to Maximos, the eschatological human transcends the difference and division into "male" (ἄρρεν/ἄρσεν) and "female" (θῆλυ) to fulfill God's plan for humanity in uniting all creation with the divine through deification. Maximos is squarely situated here within an imposing trajectory of early Christian exegetes who variously wrestled with the Genesis creation story (Gen 1–3) and with the Pauline corpus, in particular with Paul's affirmation that in Christ there is "neither male nor female" (Gal 3:28), on one hand, and with his famed Adam–Christ typology (Rom 5:12–21), on the other. Moreover, these exegetical undertakings had to be articulated from within the defining parameters of the Greek medical sciences and metaphysics of difference.

In addition to these cultural currents, Maximos distinctively exposited his understanding of sexual difference[5] through his teaching of the *logoi* of creation. The *logoi* refer to the divine ideas or designs that define the universe's diverse and individuated ontological architecture. Maximos offers one of his clearest expositions of this teaching at *Difficulty* 7.16: "Containing the preexisting *logoi* of beings before all ages, by His good will He established the visible and invisible creation out of non-being based on them, *creating* and continuing to create *with reason and wisdom all things* (Wis 9:1–2) at their necessary moment, universals as well as particulars."[6] As Maximos indicates, the *logoi*

---

[5] Sexual difference as a concept from feminist and gender studies has a long and complex tradition that is often traced to late second-wave French and Belgian feminists, especially Luce Irigaray and Monique Wittig. I do not intend to use the term with the full theoretical apparatus that originates with theorists like Irigaray and later challenged by early third-wave/queer theorists, such as Judith Butler. Rather, I primarily use sexual difference as a relatively loose category for two main reasons. First, much of this Element is itself the debate about what something such as "sexual difference" even is, and therefore its meaning needs to be allowed a certain conceptual freedom that is then attended to through a nuanced study that discourages a readymade and simple definition from the outset, a definition that would likely be unintelligible without proper context-ualization. The second reason is that "sexual difference" has now become the most commonly used term to debate the subject in Maximian studies, in part, I think, because it also approximates the Greek terminology that Maximos uses in *Difficulty* 41 better than alternatives.

[6] *Diff* 7.16. I capitalize references to the divine to avoid ambiguity in the subject antecedent.

designate both universal categories, such as existence or beauty, and specific individuals, such as Maximos and Anastasios. Given this understanding of the *logoi*, it is noteworthy that the Confessor asserts in *Difficulty* 41 that sexual differentiation into male and female contravenes God's intention, having no basis in the *logos*, and will therefore be eliminated. Simply put, sexual difference is unnatural and ephemeral.

This bold affirmation has generated a lively scholarly conversation over the past eight decades that has yielded substantively different, and sometimes diametrically opposed, interpretations. Presently I offer an overview and assessment of these interpretative traditions, but for now, I would like to register my primary reservation about the lion's share of them. Despite their ample merits, these studies evince little appreciable familiarity with scholarship on the body and sexual difference during late antiquity. Accordingly, the historiographical, if not theological, persuasiveness of their findings is at least partly compromised. The unexamined assumption that ever-so-slightly curtails my otherwise effusive appreciation of this excellent scholarship is that one can draw lines of unbroken conceptual continuity, that is, that one can assume a certain unshakeable referential stability, between late antiquity and the present regarding key terms of the debate, such as "male" and "female." I am skeptical about the self-evidence of this assumption. While there is some disagreement about models of sexual difference in antiquity and late antiquity (see section one), Roman Christians espoused fundamentally different tenets about the status of the body and the grounds of sexual difference than any modern or postmodern model. If so, Maximos' reflections on sexual difference require a systematic, contextualizing revision and reinterpretation.

Concretely, I argue that Maximos tacitly envisioned the eradication of sexual difference as female sublimation into the male, resulting in a sexually homogenized eschatology predicated on male singularity. Maximos deserves a modest concession in this regard, though: Unlike some of his predecessors, who were unapologetic and sometimes vitriolically misogynistic about this outcome, Maximos attempted to articulate human unity beyond female *and male* – he simply did not succeed in that undertaking. This failure is largely attributable to the inescapable epistemological constraints of his geochronological context, which was defined by scriptural specificity and Patristic precedent, as well as by Greek intellectual legacies. For example, Aristotle's works on sexual difference and embryology remained the standard in the seventh century, and despite discrete innovations or partial contestations by others, premodern Greek medicine perdured as an inhospitable environment to non-male bodies and was especially injurious and nasty to women. Maximos thus inherited intricate legacies of both traditions that he idiosyncratically transformed while remaining shackled by some of their operative androcentric and correlatedly misogynistic assumptions. The upshot is that the monastic author's bold and otherwise compelling vision of human unity with God never fully eschewed the trappings of sexist discourse, thereby jeopardizing the thoroughgoing coherence of his theological project, even if judged by its own logical grammar. Next, I sketch a cartography of the scholarly landscape on sexual difference in Maximian studies to situate my argument in relation to the conversations that have preceded it.

To my knowledge, Hans Urs von Balthasar was the first modern scholar to engage sexual difference in Maximos' corpus. While discussing *Difficulty* 41, von Balthasar argues for a synthesis of the two sexes that results in a transformation "of the mortal condition" (*des sterblichen Zustands*) into what he dubs a "higher third [condition] (*höherem Dritten*)"[7] that, to retain the divine image, extends Paul's Gal 3:28 to "all sexual difference (*alle geschechtliche Differenz*)" and, therefore, this difference "must be denied – primarily in a personal, but consequently also in a corporeal sphere (*leiblichen Sphäre*)."[8] Von Balthasar takes Maximos' claims about a sexless eschaton seriously by proposing a synthesis that attempts to negate sexual difference. Still, we must wonder whether this synthesis avoids the trappings of Roman masculinity discourse (see below).

By contrast, Juan-Miguel Garrigues maintained that the conception

> of birth as a manifestation of a fallen mode of being ... of human nature (*du mode d'être ... déchu de la nature humaine*) is without a doubt derivative from the theory of Gregory of Nyssa, according to which sexuality is a consequence of sin. Also, in reverse from Origenism, it is not the natural distinction of the sexes (*la distinction naturelle des sexes*) that, for Maximos, is posterior to the fall, but the *mode* of their division.[9]

Garrigues highlights Maximos' debt to Gregory and Origen in regarding sexual opposition as a postlapsarian event, but inexplicably also refers to a "natural distinction of the sexes" before the fall, a belief that, as we will see, Maximos never espoused. On Garrigues' reading, the fall only affects human relations, so that Christ's salvific effect on humanity is not directed at the "natural difference of the sexes" but at "the passionate mode of their relationships (*le mode passionnel de leurs rapports*)."[10] Because Garrigues assumes two prelapsarian "natural sexes," he surmises that Maximos never envisioned the eradication of male and female as such, only of their postlapsarian antagonism.

Following Garrigues, Doru Costache advanced the related notion that "living above gender was for him [Maximos] not a spiritual victory over the gendered

---

[7] Von Balthasar, *Kosmische Liturgie*, 203.   [8] Von Balthasar, *Kosmische Liturgie*, 202.
[9] Garrigues, *Maxime le Confesseur*, 108, emphasis of the original.
[10] Garrigues, *Maxime le Confesseur*, 178.

humankind, but instead represented the virtuous reorientation of the human energies toward dispassionate relationships."[11] Costache thus tries to resolve sexual difference on the relational, not the corporeal, plane. Similarly, Paul Blowers has taken exception to von Balthasar's notion of a sexual synthesis, underscoring that "it is not clear why the difference between male and female must absolutely evaporate in the age to come. Human 'mediation' looks toward a final dissolution, not of sexes as such, but of the alienation between sexes."[12] Here, Blowers reaffirms Costache's point that the fundamental change inaugurated by Christ between the sexes is a virtuous reorientation of their relationships, not an "evaporation" of their sexual distinctions. Kostake Milkov similarly concludes: "The journey towards the uniting of all creation, as Maximus sees it, happens through the overcoming of the divisions, but not through the abolishing of the distinctions."[13] Finally, Yekaterina Khitruk has pithily expressed the central claim of this interpretative tradition:

> Just as in overcoming the first division into created and uncreated beings (тварное и нетварное бытие) God does not cease to be God nor the human, human, so also in overcoming the last division (into the male and female sex), the human does not cease to possess the characteristics (признаками) of the one or the other sex (того или другого пола).[14]

In a word, these scholars collectively assume that Maximos presupposes sexually dimorphic bodies that endure eschatologically, while their adversity does not.

This interpretative tradition is not without hermeneutical infelicities, however. For example, in addition to the anachronistic assumption of a specific type of sexual dimorphism (see Section 1), this interpretation chimerically produces a position that Maximos nowhere articulates. That is, the Confessor never wrote about the postlapsarian brokenness of male–female relationships as such, perhaps in part because in his protology there never existed prelapsarian sexually differentiated bodies whose ideal relationships were shattered by the ancestral transgression to begin with. The closest approximations to this subject are his vaguest advice to neophyte monks to avoid spending too much time with women,[15] his mediation in the early 640s between the implacable Coptic nuns of the monastery of Sakerdos and the Alexandrian governor George,[16] and his affirmation that using women for sexual pleasure rather than for reproduction is abusive.[17] But these passages hardly constitute more than offhand remarks addressed, in all cases, to monastic recipients and cannot be aggregated to

[11] Costache, "Living above Gender," 263. [12] Blowers, *Maximus the Confessor*, 221.
[13] Milkov, "Maximus," 436. [14] Khitruk "Концептуализация отношения пола," 50.
[15] E.g., *ChL* 3.20. [16] See *Ep* 11, 18; PG 91.453A–457D; 584D–589B. [17] E.g., *ChL* 2.17.

establish a major theme in the Confessor's thought, nor do any of them appear in the context of eschatological speculation. Further, and tellingly overlooked in this interpretative current, is the fact that Maximos himself did not hesitate to invoke pseudo-Pauline literature (e.g., 1 Tim 2:12–14) in an effort to silence women who theologically disagreed with him, such as the *patrikia* Martina, widow of the emperor Herakleios and de facto Roman head of state for most of 641.[18] Simply put, there is little evidence that Maximos envisioned an eschatologically irenic outcome to male–female agonistics when writing about eradicating sexual difference.

Indeed, some scholars have already questioned interpretations that mollify Maximos' assertions about the eschatological eradication of sexual difference. For example, Karolina Kochańczyk-Bonińska was the first to contend that "I cannot agree with the suggestion that ... only the division will be dismissed but there will still be some kind of a distinction between man and woman. The entire *Difficulty* 41 should have been aborted in order to make this theory convincing."[19] More recently, David Bradshaw has also registered his skepticism: "I cannot agree with some recent exegetes who think ... that for Maximus, our physical sexual differentiation will remain in the eschaton."[20] Two other scholars have reached similar conclusions. Sotiris Mitralexis maintains, after a disciplined close reading of *Difficulty* 41, that "sexual difference *itself* (and not only sexual division or reproduction) will not endure the *eschata*."[21] Eren Brown Dewhurst concurs with this assessment, adding: "In saying that the property of male and female is in no way linked to the original *logos* of human nature, Maximus claims that male and female characteristics were never intended to be a part of human nature."[22] Accordingly, he continues: "Since sexual difference is absent from human *logos* and will be completely removed, both in difference and division, we can see it better typifying an instance of a change introduced into *tropos* that is anticipated to be removed from humanity eschatologically."[23]

In the previous passage, Dewhurst is invoking a famed distinction in Maximos' thought between *logos* and *tropos* that we must board before going further.[24] The *logos*, as noted before, corresponds to the divine conception of an

---

[18] *Ep* 12, PG 91:461C–464A. See Salés, "Maximos' Correspondence" (forthcoming).

[19] Kochańczyk-Bonińska, "Maximus' Concept of the Sexes," 237; similarly see Bradshaw, "Sexual Difference," 27.

[20] Bradshaw, "Sexual Difference," 27.

[21] Mitralexis, "Attempt at Clarifying," 199 (emphasis the author's).

[22] Dewhurst, "Absence of Sexual Difference," 206; see also 220–221.

[23] Dewhurst, "Absence of Sexual Difference," 212.

[24] On the *logos-tropos* distinction, see Larchet, "La conception maximienne," 276–284 and *La divinisation*, 62–80, 141–151, and 617–624; Mira, "El doblete ΛΟΓΟΣ- ΤΡΟΠΟΣ," 685–696; Thunberg, *Microcosm and Mediator*, 442–444; Mitralexis, "Maximus' 'Logical' Ontology," 65–82; Tollefsen, *Christocentric Cosmology*, 64–81.

individual's existential parameters, while the *tropos* (or, in full, τρόπος τῆς ὑπάρξεως/*tropos tes hyparxeos*, meaning mode of existence) signifies an individual's concrete way of living out those parameters. Dewhurst perceptively references this distinction to argue that sexual difference is not divinely encoded in human nature but has been modally invented by humans themselves; thus, it is not an essential predicate, and thus, cannot be a prelapsarian human attribute. Dewhurst concludes that Maximos envisions the eschatological end of sexual difference itself: "Unlike other divisions, when it comes to male and female, both the division and the difference itself are to be removed."[25] In sum, this last interpretative approach contests the work of earlier scholars who question the eschatological elimination of sexual difference as such. This Element highlights further, however, the doubtless disturbing and as of yet unexplored implications of this last interpretation against the Confessor's cultural backdrop.

Quite apart from these rival interpretations, Lars Thunberg understood Maximos as implying that overcoming sexual difference in Christ "is not effected by the elimination of anything which is human, and which therefore pertains to man or woman."[26] Instead, he situates this conversation within a larger late ancient current of thought that often psychologized the sexes, equating masculinity with the thymetic faculty (θυμός/*thymos*) and femininity with the epithymetic faculty (ἐπιθυμία/*epithymia*) of the soul. Thunberg makes a partly compelling case that Maximos' understanding of sexual difference can operate in these metaphorical registers: By containing sexual difference to a purely psychological dimension, Thunberg transpositions the removal of sexual difference from the body to the soul. Read thus, the elimination of "male and female" only refers to the taming of the nonrational faculties by reason (λόγος/*logos* or νοῦς/*nous*). Therefore, Maximos never meant that men and women as such would cease to exist. More recently, Adam Cooper has restated this position, adding to Thunberg's original claim that "the reconciliation or union between male and female does not require the abolition of physical distinction but is primarily a matter of knowledge and will."[27] Cooper joins Thunberg in preserving the anatomical distinction of the sexes by relegating eschatological changes to a nonphysical dimension.

Granted, Thunberg and Cooper are correct in suggesting that Maximos gestured to the tradition that metaphorically used sexual difference to refer to

---

[25] Dewhurst, "Absence of Sexual Difference," 217.

[26] Thunberg, *Microcosm and Mediator*, 379. Larchet does not engage the question of sexual difference in *La divinisation*, even though he cites the passage in question here. See Larchet, *La divinisation*, 111, as well as 201–202.

[27] Cooper, *Holy Flesh, Wholly Deified*, 222. See also Thunberg's discussion, *Microcosm and Mediator*, 151–154, 180–207.

the soul. But their psychologizing thesis (based largely on *Thalassios* 48) does not account for several passages, especially in *Difficulty* 41, where the Confessor is unambiguously referring to sexed people with reproductive capabilities. Further, this interpretation of sexual difference itself mimics the structure of male and female sublimation into an ostensibly ungendered superior state upon which, however, masculinity yet again reinscribes itself. Consider, for example, that male and female, which stand for drive (θυμός) and desire (ἐπιθυμία), are subordinated to reason (λόγος), a concept, besides its grammatically male gender, inextricable from masculinity discourse. If so, this interpretation has two shortcomings: First, its heuristic value is circumscribed by its fractional explanation of the evidence; second, the operative metaphor itself mirrors the same committedly androcentric-signifying economy that anticipates the eschatological erasure of the female. In other words, how is it possible to dissociate discourses about gendered bodies from discourses about gendered metaphors as if these somehow did not emerge from the same culture or as if they were not mutually reinforcing vectors in service of androcentric functions? A brief survey of the precedent for this metaphorical interpretation predictably indicates the coimplication of both discourses, not their mutual exclusivity.

The psychologizing tendency first identified by Thunberg can be imagistically traced to Plato's famed analogy of the charioteer of *Phaidros* 246a, but it flourished in the writings of later exegetes well-known to, and often cited by, Maximos. For example, Philo of Alexandria tells us in *On Husbandry* 73 that "Desire and irascibility are horses, the one male, the other female."[28] Doubtless, Philo is referring to a psychologically stereotyping sense here, but that hardly means he never extended this form of stereotyping beyond psychological semantics. In *Questions and Responses on Exodus*, a text only preserved whole in an Armenian translation, Philo justifies that the "male" (արու) possesses greater perfection by referencing the infamous passage in Aristotle's *On the Generation of Animals* 775a that describes the female as an incomplete male.[29] Indeed, of the few Greek fragments that survive of this same work, Philo expressly references this Peripatetic subtext by seemingly agreeing with natural philosophers "that the female is nothing other than an unfinished (ἀτελὲς) male."[30] Philo is no longer talking about psychological metaphors but about Aristotelian embryology and the concomitant devaluation of female bodies.

---

[28] Philo, *On Husbandry* 73. Philo makes similar claims in numerous places, including *On the Contemplative Life* 60–63; *On Drunkenness* 59–61, and most expressly in the surviving Armenian translation of his *Questions and Responses on Exodus* 1.8, Aucher, ed. See further, MacDonald, *There Is No Male and Female*, 99; Conway, *Behold the Man*, 51; Lipsett, *Desiring Conversion*, 11–12; Constas, trans., *On Difficulties in Sacred Scripture*, 270, n. 13.

[29] *Questions and Responses on Exodus*, 1.8, ed. Aucher, p. 451.

[30] *Frag.* 1.7a, in *Questions on Genesis and Exodus*, ed. Petit.

We find a similar dynamic in the writings of Clement of Alexandria, whom the Confessor also knew well and cited by name.[31] As with Philo, Clement's use of psychologizing metaphors about sexual difference did not exempt him from making prejudicial affirmations about female bodily "weakness" and overall inferiority by comparison to the "more perfect" male body; such statements abound in his texts and he expresses them unabashedly.[32] Granted, he affirms the equality of the soul between men and women but somehow adds in the same breath that women's "inferior" bodily constitution destines them for childbearing and housekeeping, especially since men are superior "in all things."[33] While distasteful to egalitarian sensitivities, this form of blatant male supremacy in a late ancient Roman author's writings is hardly an earth-shattering discovery. Rather, it is epistemologically discombobulating to suppose that ancient authors would have engaged in gender stereotyping when speaking about the soul but would have held back when speaking about bodily difference. Further late ancient Christian authors who engaged in this kind of psychologizing discourse could be discussed, but these examples should sufficiently illustrate my point.[34]

So, for Thunberg's and Cooper's psychological interpretation to be wholly compelling, it must demonstrate at least two points: First, that Maximos somehow substantively broke with the hierarchization of this metaphorical tradition, and second, that he only ever used a metaphorical register when speaking about sexual difference. But the evidence supports neither point. I address the second point at length in Section 2, but the short of it is that Maximos concretely writes in *Difficulty* 41 about the eschatological overcoming of women and men with sexed bodies and reproductive capabilities, not just about "male" and "female." Conversely, three passages in Maximos' corpus are relevant to the first point.

The first passage appears in the *Commentary on the Lord's Prayer*, where the monastic exegete explains that the meek and humble are said to bear the "configuration" (μορφή) of Christ by the Spirit, and in this configuration, he concludes, "the divine apostle says, 'there is not male and female,' that is, drive and desire."[35] Maximos continues, adding that by moving, living, and having one's being in Christ (cf. Acts 17:28), one no longer "bears in himself, as though 'male and female,' the opposing dispositions of these passions, as I said, so that

---

[31] E.g., *Diff* 7.24.

[32] E.g., *Stromateis*, 3.2.6–8; 3.13.92–93; 4.8.59.4–5; see also 6.12.100.3 and 6.16.139.3. Compare with Dunning, *Specters of Paul*, 51–74 for a discussion of Clement on sexual difference and his discursive failure to present a fully coherent picture of a unified anthropology. For Clement's possible echo in *Thalassios*, see Constas, *On Difficulties in Scripture*, 270 n. 13.

[33] E.g., *Stromateis*, 4.8.60.1.

[34] Thunberg is also aware of Evagrios of Pontos' *Praktikos*, 1.63, where a similar use of psychological metaphors appears, as well as Gregory of Nyssa's *On Virginity*, ed. Jaeger, 325.

[35] *Comm*, ll. 340–343.

reason (λόγος) is not enslaved to them."[36] It is apparent in these passages that the ascetic thinker is replicating the same connection between male/drive and female/desire that we had already seen in Philo and Clement, while again subordinating them to the male-coded *logos*, here conveniently interchangeable with Christ. The second passage occurs in *Thalassios* 48.5. Here, Maximos claims that "[Christ] unified the human, mystically removing the difference of male and female by the spirit, rendering free the *logos* of nature as pertains to both (ἐπ' ἀμφοῖν) from the distinctive features (ἰδιωμάτων) that are in the passions."[37] I agree with Maximos Constas, who notes that male and female function here as "symbolic expressions of the passionate parts of the soul."[38] Nonetheless, the logic of the passage elevates these two non-rational faculties into a higher state that is, once again, the male-coded *logos*. Specifically, reason (*logos*) functions here as a double entendre that refers both to the higher mental faculty, always already legible as masculine, and to the Word of God, Christ. If so, masculinity and femininity are not both overcome in this metaphorical architecture so long as the male remains; rather, the female alone appears to be subsumed. Most telling of this last point is the third relevant passage, *Questions and Doubts* 57, where Maximos no longer identifies men with drive, but with reason (*logos*), and equates women with desire and animals with drive. Therefore, even if the male and female are ostensibly "resolved" into a higher state within this psychological metaphor, that highest and final state is clearly male-coded. The upshot is female erasure within a phallogocentric symbolic economy, not the categorical transcendence of sex as such.[39] In sum, the metaphorical interpretation is a welcome discovery of Maximos' use of prior traditions that psychologized sexual difference, but it does not account for texts where the Confessor has the unsexing of sexed bodies in view, nor does it obviate the problem of the metaphorical hierarchization of sexual difference that elides the female in favor of the male; indeed, the latter structure is predictive and epitomic of the former.

Finally, some scholars have taken yet different approaches by proposing spiritualizing or constructive projects. Elder Aimilianos of Simonopetra interprets Maximos' affirmation that dispassionate people no longer recognize the difference between male and female as referring to the ability not to be affected by this, or any other, characteristic of human otherness: "He [the dispassionate man] has no particular awareness of gender, which he has moved beyond,

---

[36] *Comm*, ll. 383–386.   [37] *Thal* 48.5.   [38] Constas, *Difficulties in Scripture*, 270, n. 13.

[39] This term is a neologism coined by Derrida in his famed essay "La pharmacie de Platon," 256–367. For an English version, see Derrida, *Dissemination*, 61–171. It has since been picked up extensively by feminist and queer theorists. See, for example, Butler, *Gender Trouble*, ix, 9–19, 26–32 and *Bodies That Matter*, 36–37, 48–52.

because all men and women to him are like angels."[40] While in the rest of his commentary Elder Aimilianos maintains sexual dimorphism, he de-emphasizes it in his analysis by shifting the focus to spiritual perception, which he regards as somehow blind to sexual difference. Conversely, Ashley Purpura has promisingly pondered whether Maximos' teachings on virtue might not open up an avenue for legitimating the broader inclusion of Orthodox women into the clergy, particularly as the virtues can level character and spiritual differences between women and men that theoretically transcend or supersede any sexual specificity and the clerical restrictions predicated on it.[41] Finally, Cameron Partridge highlighted the importance of Maximos' understanding of sexual difference beyond cis-heterobinary sexual identities, but that idea, intimidated in a doctoral thesis, has not received further elaboration in published form.[42] I concur with the ethical motivations that drive some of these studies, but I believe that constructive projects can often be sharpened further by discovering untapped possibilities that form within the logical fissures that a fine-grained reading of ancient texts can detect. I return to this matter in the conclusion of this study, so I table for now the discussion of these constructive possibilities.

Now, for a summary of the foregoing scholarly cartography. Von Balthasar's suggestion of a sexual synthesis has been effectively abandoned. Conversely, there is historiographical merit to some aspects of Thunberg's and Cooper's interpretative framework but also important limitations. A few constructive projects have also been proposed that find unexplored possibilities for contemporary discussions surrounding gender, sexuality, and sexual difference in Maximos' writings. Finally, the majority position, which argues for some form of eschatological reconciliation between the sexes, has been disputed by several scholars who maintain that sexual difference itself vanishes in the eschaton. I believe this last tradition is correct in doubling down on the eschatological eradication of sexual difference, but it stops short of recognizing the troubling conclusions that insinuate themselves when Maximos is read with greater awareness of his context.

Specifically, Maximos' claims stand on a determinedly sexist hierarchization of corporeal difference that regarded all but apex males as categorically inferior beings. So, eliminating sexual difference in Maximos' milieu meant something quite different than it does, for example, among those poststructuralist articulations of gender theory that propose a non-hierarchical fluid spectrum of gender identities. For Roman intellectuals with Maximos' formation, eliminating sexual difference almost certainly referred to tacit sublimation of non-males into

---

[40] Elder Aimilianos of Simonopetra, *Mystical Marriage*, 159.

[41] For the whole argument, see Purpura, *God, Hierarchy, Power*, 54–78.

[42] See Partridge, "Transfiguring Sexual Difference," 118–229.

idealized male singularity. In other words, the dynamics and presuppositions behind those dynamics were not what Bradshaw calls an "underlying ontology in which people at their core are asexual beings,"[43] but one in which everyone is either a man or what Jonathan Walters calls "unmen,"[44] that is, everyone who is not yet, never will be, or can no longer be considered a man.

This anthropology is an extension of what I call "androprimacy," a neologism that I explain in detail in the first section, which situates Maximos in the Greek medical tradition and in the disputed legacies of scriptural and Patristic interpretations of sexual difference. The second section reexamines *Difficulty* 41 in light of the androprimacy lens I propose, according to which sexual difference is only effected by sublimating female into male. The third section broadens the discussion to Maximos' larger corpus by analyzing texts where Maximos' commitment to androprimacy in his exegesis of Eve and Mary compromises his theological vision. The conclusion revisits some of the impasses exposed in the course of this study, assesses where that leaves the scholarly conversation, and hints at ways forward for constructive projects with feminist and queer sensitivities. In penning this study, I hope to encourage seasoned and aspiring Maximian scholars alike to further emulate the Confessor's penchant for retrieving the contemporary significance of ancient texts by leading out – *ex-egeting* – the vast hermeneutical possibilities embedded within them.

1 Androprimacy and the Sexed Body in Late Antiquity

This section examines the legacies surrounding the body and sexual difference that Maximos inherited and how they coalesced into what I call "androprimacy." I coined this neologism to name a pervasive social structure that flourished in most ancient societies and that arguably remains in large part the global norm today.[45] By androprimacy I mean the implicit or explicit belief in male precedence, however conceived and deployed, across every register: corporeal, temporal, political, intellectual, religious, ontological, moral, and so on. In coining this term for historiographical purposes, I intend no anachronistic interpolations, but an analytical lens to aid modern readers identify structures of power predicated on sexually differentiated bodies. That is, I do not mean to reify an essence but to make a dynamic vector of socio-discursive power apparent to contemporary audiences. As an analytical concept, androprimacy is cut of the same cloth as other well-worn concepts of gender theory, such as androcentrism, andronormativity, misogyny, and patriarchy (which I also use in my analysis here), but it names a different type of attitude and

---

[43] Bradshaw, "Sexual Difference," 30.   [44] Walters, "Invading the Roman Body," 33.
[45] See further, Salés, "Androprimacy," 195–213.

social structure not fully captured by these concepts, even if it closely intersects with them. Androprimacy results in the systemic devaluation of and stratified adversity for everyone who falls short of idealized conceptions of masculinity. Androprimacy is thus inseparable from its concomitant belief in male suprem-acy; indeed, androprimacy refers to male supremacy as much as it does to priority – the two are discursively coincident.

In the premodern sources at issue here, androprimacy largely appears to be axiomatic, not propositional; it is a premise, not an argument, and its effects can often be felt a posteriori. To illustrate, consider the uses of androprimacy in the Pauline/pseudo-Pauline corpus. In 1 Cor 11, the Corinthians appear to use the logic of androprimacy (11:3–10) – much to Paul's disapproval (11:11–16) – to explain why men need not cover their heads when praying and prophesying, while women should: "For man did not come from woman, but woman from man" (v. 8). Here, the mere hint at Adam's corporeal and temporal primacy over Eve allows the Corinthians to conclude a few lines later that "therefore, a woman should have authority upon her head" (11:10). The logical structure is that if the male came first, the subordinate status of the female follows. Nowhere do the Corinthians legitimate *that* the male was first, or why temporal or corporeal primacy is somehow a suitable benchmark for determining social status to begin with; they simply assume that temporal and corporeal andropri-macy sufficiently justifies female subordination. Similarly so in 1 Tim 2:12–13, where pseudo-Paul cites androprimacy to silence women: "I do not allow a woman to teach or to exert authority over a man; she must be quiet, given that Adam was made first, then Eve." Again, androprimacy here functions as a premise that needs only to be conjured up to magically compel women into silence.

I sincerely hope that "androprimacy" becomes a helpful analytic and descrip-tive term for feminism and gender studies more broadly, but for the purposes of this Element, I would like to trace the antecedents and subsequent congeal-ing of what we may specifically call Greco-Roman Christian androprimacy, that is, a concrete type of androprimacy developed by Greek-speaking Roman Christians. This background is vital to fleshing out the fuller implications of the eschatological demise of sexual difference as Maximos likely envisioned it. Accordingly, there are two major goals in this section. The first is to follow the development of Greek medical anthropology from Aristotle to Maximos to determine what anatomical model of sexual difference the Confessor presup-posed. The second is to foreground the so-called "myth of the primal androgyne" and its Greek Patristic reception.

These two traditions converged long before Maximos and are readily dis-cernible in his own writings, so there should be no controversy in suggesting that he should be understood as actively engaging with them. Concretely,

I highlight some of the tensions that emerged from the coalescence of these currents. Despite considerable sexual fluidity predicated on the materiality of the body, Aristotelian-flavored medical discourses about sexual difference ultimately did impose a boundary between male and female that could never be fully crossed – not, at any rate, under the naturalistic lineaments they presupposed and certainly not in this earthly life (which was the only life in Aristotelian philosophy). If so, then, how to reconcile such a view of the sexually differentiated body with later Christian thought inspired largely by Paul that anticipated eschatological unity presumably beyond sexual difference (e.g., Gal 3:28)? Compounding the problem further, Paul's own thinking on the subject elsewhere favors the androprimal and androtelic Adam–Christ typology (Rom 5:12–21), which is itself likely inextricable from Greco-Roman views of the ideal male body as the metric of perfection. When pressed on the crux of the matter, Christian intellectuals before Maximos struggled to articulate the eschatological space of the non-male body.

The Confessor was no exception in this regard. Admittedly, he produced a creative and highly idiosyncratic response to these anatomical and exegetical tensions, but one that, even if judged by its own logic, is not without inconsistencies. The reason is that the overcoming of sexual difference as Maximos would articulate it was necessarily already plagued by the androprimacy implicit in both Greek medical discourse and Paul's Adam–Christ typology. The upshot, then, was a predictable concession: positing a human universality constructed along eschatologically attainable male lineaments wherein the non-male fits poorly, perhaps not at all. I doubt that Maximos and others of his exegetical persuasion regarded this step as a concession at all, though. For the problem with androprimacy's axiomatic status is that it is not a proposition one assents to but a culturally normalized premise whose power for social formation is proportional to its imperceptibility. This is why it must be named.

Androprimacy, the One-Sex Body, and Greek Medical Anthropology

Maximos' androprimacy was partly contingent on medical models of sexual difference going back to classical antiquity and that have only recently been incorporated into the conversation on sexual difference in Maximian studies. Vladimir Cvetković published an excellent study that reviews a few early Christian views on gender, including the Confessor's. He argues that during Maximos' time, the "difference between man and woman was not expressed on the basis of sex and gender, but in relation to the 'one-sex' model."[46]

---

[46] Cvetković. "Sex," 163.

Cvetković's identification of the one-sex model is the first study on the ascetic thinker that mentions this key term in scholarship on Greco-Roman gender, even if he takes the applicability of that term in a different direction than I suggest here.

Cvetković footnotes the one-sex model to Stephanie Cobb's work on early Christian female martyrs,[47] but it originates earlier, with Thomas Laqueur's *Making Sex*. Laqueur explores ancient conceptions of the body in the Mediterranean basin and their reception through Freud, skipping, however, the entire medieval Roman era. In his controversial study, Laqueur proposes that the Greeks and their heirs operated under the conceptual aegis of a one-sex model that presupposes a single basic body that functions on a fluid, vertical scale oriented toward masculinity, rather than positing two essentially different and incommensurable bodies as in modernist inventions of sexual dimorphism.

Although Laqueur's work has redefined the field of premodern Mediterranean conceptions of sex, it has not been without some committed detractors.[48] The most relevant of these is Helen King's book-length critique, tellingly called *The One-Sex Body on Trial*. King revisits the Greek accounts of Phaethousa and Agnodike that formed the backbone of Laqueur's argument for antiquity and its reception in early modern Western Europe and offers a competing interpretation of the evidence.[49] These two Greek individuals were assigned female at birth, but during their adult years began a rapid and ultimately lethal transition to masculinity. Laqueur argued that these transitions betrayed belief in a single body shared by women and men, within which sexual difference functioned as a relatively free-flowing variable. In broadest brushstrokes, King's argument contests this claim by noting, first, that both women in fact *failed* to become men and, second, by incorporating some evidence that hints at the synchronous existence of a two-sex model that Laqueur overlooked. King concludes that Laqueur's argument that the two-sex model first originated in the eighteenth century owing to a desire to fix male and female biology on reliable essences that displaced a previously universal one-sex model is untenable. Instead, she maintains that the two models have coexisted in various tense permutations since antiquity.

For the purposes of this study, though, this debate has some significant limitations. For example, with the exception of brief nods to Galen and Nemesios,[50] these studies effectively overlook the entire medical corpus

---

[47] Cobb, *Dying to Be Men*, 5.
[48] Cadden, *Meanings of Sex Difference*; Green, "Bodily Essences," 149–171, 264–268. See also Betancourt, *Byzantine Intersectionality*, 230, n. 77.
[49] King, *The One-Sex Body on Trial*.
[50] See King, *One-Sex Body*, 2; Laqueur, *Making Sex*, 4.

produced by Grecophone Romans between late antiquity and the Palaiologan era. Thus, King's critique of Laqueur has little appreciable bearing on scholarly assumptions that Maximos held to a model of sexual dimorphism. That is all the more so because even the two-sex model of antiquity – such as it might have been – should not be conflated with modern versions of sexual dimorphism, often presupposed by contemporary Maximian scholars.[51] Further, King does not categorically deny the existence of the one-sex model, but Laqueur's implication that it was the sole option available until the eighteenth century.[52] So, King's criticism is rightly directed at Laqueur's lack of localized nuance, which in turn helps him promote a somewhat specious and low-resolution grand narrative that loses explanatory value when pressed on specifics. Conversely, why must we assume the non-self-evident premise that Maximos believed in a two-sex model when most of the relevant scholarship on Roman gender suggests that that would be highly unlikely? On this point, Kathryn Ringrose's words are rightly cautionary: "The Byzantines perceived the body as malleable, able to be changed to suit the needs of society … Within the Byzantine world, the boundaries between gender categories were very flexible, with the result that it is difficult today to define [them] … using western terminology."[53] Instead, she suggests that by looking at the texts on their own terms, we can identify a varied number of what she calls "intermediate gender categories."[54] I concur with Ringrose's assessment on the whole, and therefore prioritize an exposition of the intellectual genealogies of sexual difference as the Confessor inherited and transformed them to accord him the localized nuance he deserves.

For this reason, I jettison for now the debate about the one-sex or two-sex model in favor of what I call a model of Greco-Roman Christian androprimacy. I think this model approximates the Confessor's conceptual parameters better and allows greater analytical flexibility when faced with complex sources. For example, I found in my reading of the texts that by the seventh century the almost exclusively medical focus assumed by both Laqueur and King would become hermeneutically restrictive. The reason is that for someone like Maximos the body was no longer solely a medical subject (it was that too) but a theological subject, and its theologically-inflected ontology had all-too-real consequences for it as a physiological entity. Even so, Maximos' physical understanding of the body was still indebted to the medical traditions debated by Laqueur and King. I am fairly confident that Maximos presupposed a heavily modified version of Laqueur's one-sex body model (see below), yet

---

[51] Consult, for example, Soranos, *On Gynaecology*, 3.1. For commentary, Holmes, *Gender*, 38–41.
[52] See especially King, *One-Sex Body*, 3–12, 31–48.   [53] Ringrose, "Byzantine Body," 362.
[54] Ringrose, "Byzantine Body," 363.

consistent with androprimacy. From that vantage point, the Confessor certainly conceived of the body and sexual difference as mutable and non-essential.

Maximos partly owed this conception to the works of Plato and Aristotle, but for now, I focus on Aristotle's medical anthropology specifically and its permutations during late antiquity. Simply speaking, Aristotle believed that the default newborn should be male given two axioms he considered self-evident: first, that the male alone provides seed with animating potential, and second, that like should beget like.[55] Naturally, Aristotle's system is driven by androprimal assumptions, as it presupposes the formal precedence of the male over the female, rendering masculinity the human default. Androprimacy thus grounds andronormativity. Still, for Aristotle both parents determine the newborn's sex: the father as producing seed, the mother as providing matter.[56] According to this logic, the newborn's sex resulted from accidents that accompanied the process of gestation, and especially of the so-called "vital heat," which for the Stagirite radiates from the heart and determines not whether the newborn is male or female but rather how closely the newborn approximates an idealized masculinity.[57] Hence the notion that classical Greek sexual difference is not a simple and straightforward binary but a vertical manward spectrum.

Aristotle famously details the process of embryology and its attendant circumstances in *Generation of Animals*. As mentioned, an embryo's sex depends on the heart's vital heat, which constitutes the "principle (ἀρχή) and cause (αἰτία) of the female and male" (*GA* 766b4–5). In other words, for Aristotle the seed does not pre-contain information that determines sexual specifics analogous to chromosomal combinations. Rather,

> the semen of the male ... has in itself a principle of such a type as to elicit movement and entirely to concoct the ultimate nourishment, while the female's semen contains matter only. If the former prevails, it brings the latter to itself; but if it is dominated, it changes into its opposite or otherwise goes into extinction.[58]

The male seed directs the fetus' development in the direction of masculinity because it alone has the necessary internal principle for achieving this result. But if heat is lacking, the overwhelming materiality of the female "semen"[59]

---

[55] For further primary sources on this subject, see Hippokrates, *Nature of the Child*, 11; Aristotle, *On the Generation of Animals*, 729a11; Soranos of Ephesos, *Gynecologia*, 1.36, 39, 45; Galen, *On Fetal Formation* 661, 666, 668; Compare with Nemesios of Emesa, *On the Nature of the Human*, 5, 25. For a superb overview, see Wilberding, *Forms, Souls, and Embryos*; Connell, *Aristotle on Women*, especially 3–12.

[56] For an overview, see Holmes, *Gender*, 14–75.   [57] See Holmes, *Gender*, 29.

[58] *GA* 766b14–18.

[59] By this, Aristotle meant something akin to menstrual blood, which he often calls a "flow" (of blood) for short.

overcomes the male seed and yields a female body that lacks that full-spirited masculine principle, or, if it strays further from masculinity, it becomes nonviable and dies.

Aristotle is not speaking about an inflexible sex binary here but about gradients, where the bottom of the scale is not a separate form but the same form with inferior status. Holmes clarifies this idea with her characteristic lucidity: "Aristotle holds that any species (*eidos*) falling under the genus (*genos*) of animals encompasses both the male and the female. Therefore, the sexes *cannot* differ in their essence without violating Aristotle's definition of a species (*eidos*), even as they embody the contraries 'male' and 'female.'"[60] Instead, Aristotle attributes the wide-ranging sexual spectrum that encompasses males and females to environmental variables that influence gestation in particular, such as the age of the parents, the relative "fluidity" or "solidity" of their bodies, and so on.[61] Thus, the degree of vital heat of the parents determines the likelihood of yielding the "ideal" outcome: the male. However, the physical constitution of the parents is not entirely responsible for the outcome of embryos' sexual specifics either, for the latter are also impacted by environmental conditions: The Peripatetic refers to the direction the wind is blowing or to the stage of the moon as factors that influence human bodies and therefore embryonic gestation.[62]

Following this reasoning, Aristotle infamously expresses the ontological inferiority of female bodies while affirming their procreative non-expendability:

> Anyone not taking after his parents is really in a way an aberration, as herein nature has somewhat strayed from the generic type. The first beginning of this straying is when a female is formed instead of a male, even if this is a necessity required by nature, as the type of creatures separated into male and female must be kept in existence.[63]

This affirmation has been rightly criticized by feminist historians of philosophy not only for its patent misogyny but also for its logical inconsistencies.[64] How can something that naturally occurs be simultaneously an aberration and necessary? Regardless of its logical and ethical woes, this idea went on to have a long reach in the Grecophone medical sciences and can still be perceived in the thought of Maximos and his predecessors (see Section 3). What matters for now about this idea is that it grounded the belief that the human default is male.

---

[60] Holmes, *Gender*, 42–43.   [61] *GA* 766b29–34.   [62] *GA* 766b35–767a10.

[63] *GA* 767b4–12.

[64] Predictably, there is a great debate about Aristotle's views of women generally, and specifically in *Generation of Animals*. See Tress, "Metaphysical Science," 31–50.

In sum, Aristotle's system of sexual difference does not yield an incommensurable binary pre-programmed in human nature. Rather, his model might be envisioned as a single, vertical axis along which bodies move to approximate or distance themselves from the normalized male body that he calls "generic." The reason, as mentioned earlier, is that for the Peripatetic, there exists no ontological principle of "male" or "female" because the species is male by default. He clarifies this belief in the *Metaphysics*: "It might be asked why woman does not differ from man in species, given that the female and the male are opposites and difference is contrariety."[65] A few lines later, he explains that the difference is solely in matter (ὕλη), not in form (εἴδει), but species are differentiated by distinctions of form or definition, not by the specifics of matter.[66] Thus, there is no genus of "male" or "female," to which human bodies belong; there is only the species "human," comprising individuals whose differences are material, not formal.

Accordingly, there is no enduring ontological principle for Aristotle that fixes the sex of an individual; it is wholly the result of accidents attending the materiality of the body, which in turn renders sex itself dynamic and variable, even if it is within an androprimally hierarchized spectrum. Thus, as Aristotle theorized sexual difference, anything other than the ideal male *is* sexual difference *from the ideal male* and amounts to a fortuitous infelicity lower down on the ontological spectrum. Holmes adds a cautionary note, however: "None of this means that Aristotle sees embodied sex as completely fluid. If we want to understand his views on sexual difference, we have to learn to hold together the idea of fixity *and* the idea of fluidity."[67] In Aristotle's model, the female may ascend to some degree toward masculinity but may never become fully male because she is ontologically incapable of producing sufficient heat by any potentialities that inhere in her being.[68]

By contrast, the male was constantly at risk of becoming unmanly, for, much as today, masculinity was a frail status in antiquity. The Stagirite's once arcane ruminations on the nature of the body and sexual difference came to dominate social dynamics in Greco-Roman culture, particularly at the elite level. In practice, this meant that the mutability of men's bodies required constant monitoring, as Peter Brown has vividly described:

> Each man trembled forever on the brink of becoming "womanish." His flickering heat was an uncertain force. If it was to remain effective, its momentum had to be consciously maintained. It was never enough to be male: a man had to strive to remain "virile." He had to learn to exclude from his character and from the poise and temper of his body all telltale traces of "softness" that might betray, in him, the half-formed state of a woman.[69]

---

[65] *Met* 10.9, 1058a29–31.   [66] *Met* 10.9, 1058a37–1058b6.   [67] Holmes, *Gender*, 44.
[68] Holmes, *Gender*, 44.   [69] Brown, *Body and Society*, 11.

These kinds of cultural conditions were predicated on the assumption that the body was precisely the kind of thing that could "backslide" toward femininity. In this we again see the recurrent Aristotelian theme that the body primarily differs not in essence or kind but in material accidents subject to alteration.

So far, we have focused on the classical Aristotelian material, but what about the centuries closer to Maximos? Currently, the bulk of scholarship on sex and Greco-Roman culture tends to cluster around the New Testament era through the fourth century and again during the Makedonian (867–1056) and Komnenian (1081–1185) dynasties. Thus, cultural understandings of sexual difference leading up to and during Maximos' period remain relatively understudied, and the studies that do exist, mostly of medical anthropology, are often siloed off from theological materials, so we must close that gap in some humble measure here.

The late ancient Roman Empire produced numerous outstanding physicians, including the famed Galen and Nemesios, but also Aretaios of Kappadokia (fl. second century), Soranos of Ephesos (fl. second century), Metrodora of Egypt (third–sixth century?), Aetios of Amida (fl. sixth century), and two of Maximos' contemporaries, Alexandros of Tralles (ca. 525–605) and Paulos of Aigina (ca. 625–690). A review of the pertinent evidence in these physicians' texts indicates that although the practice of medicine had drastically improved since Aristotle, the paradigms of medical anthropology had remained largely unchanged. Most of these physicians were more concerned with practical solutions to medical problems than with pondering their patients' ontology. This much is apparent in the type of medical literature produced during this time, specifically, the *syllogai*,[70] which were a type of practical physician manual that possibly traced its origin to Metrodora of Egypt.[71] These medical texts permit us to extrapolate much about the medical anthropology of the time by examining assumptions in courses of treatment, as Larisa Vilimonović suggests: "Philosophy and medicine were inextricably linked . . . and the philosophy of human nature influenced the interpretation of diseases and conception of health."[72] If so, we can often extract an operative philosophy of human nature from medical procedures without the medical manuals themselves spelling out their anthropological assumptions. And by this metric, it appears that only small shifts occurred in the medical conceptualization of the body and sex and their malleability between Aristotle and Maximos.

Indeed, nearly all of the aforementioned physicians assumed that the standard of care had to be based on the male body and scaled downward for those who fell short of that ideal. For example, Alexandros of Tralles casually mentions

---

[70] Odorico, "La cultura della ΣΥΛΛΟΓΗ," 12, n. 25.
[71] See further, Storti, "Metrodora's Work," 89–110.
[72] Vilimonović, "Gender, Diseases, and Sexuality," 1203–1224, here 1206.

that "eunuchs, children, women, and those like them (ὁμοίοις τούτων)" are "weaker and softer in constitution (ἀσθενεστέρα καὶ μαλακωτέρα τὴν ἕξιν)" and therefore require medication that takes their frailer state (in comparison to men's) into account.[73] His prescription might be pragmatic, but it also shows a medical anthropology that presumes the two categories noted in the introduction, men and "unmen," where the latter is a heterogeneous group comprising eunuchs, children, women, and "those like them," who tellingly cannot be treated in the same way as men. We find the same assumption in the prescriptions of Aetios of Amida, who refers to "women, children, and others of soft bodies (μαλακῶν σωμάτων)" as similarly needing gradated recipes in relation to the male standard.[74]

Medical texts from late antiquity also continue the classical assumption that men have greater vital heat and women, eunuchs, the elderly, and children are colder. For this reason, Aetios warns readers about giving women medicines that cool down the body, since "I know many women who died from their heads getting excessively cold (ἐκ τοῦ καταψυχθῆναι τὴν κεφαλὴν) due to these medicines, and they especially affect (βλάπτονται) those who have a colder mixture (αἱ ψυχροτέραν τὴν κρᾶσιν ἔχουσαι)."[75] The phrase "those who have a colder mixture" signals a more expansive category than a male–female binary – that is, "unmen." Similarly, Aetios attributes the reproductive woes of couples to a problem with the heat of either the male or female or both. Alternatively, he suggests it might be due to the corporeal immaturity of the couple, so that women should be no younger than eighteen to reproduce, and men no younger than thirty.[76] In a similar vein, Paulos of Aigina remarks that men are particularly liable to the disease known as satyriasis due to their excess heat.[77] Here, Paulos manifestly presupposes Aristotle's belief that men are "hotter."

Indeed, there were many norms of proper masculinity among the Grecophone Romans during late antiquity that simultaneously signal its vulnerability and social stylization. Aretaios of Kappadokia lists some of these norms: "A man with healthy semen is warm, his joints work well, he is hairy, he has a good voice and a pleasant demeanor, is strong, smart, and active, and is readily recognizable as a man."[78] But with this ideal came the possibility of failing to embody masculinity. Therefore, Soranos could echo, as others would, Aristotle's dictum that the female is an unfinished male with a certain trepidation about what that might mean for men.[79] For after all, it was precisely the fact

---

[73] Alexandros of Tralles, *Therapeutics*, vol. 2:127, ll. 12–14.
[74] Aetios, *Book of Medicine*, 2.49, ll. 12–13.   [75] Aetios, *Book of Medicine*, 6.58, ll. 7–10.
[76] Aetios, *Book of Medicine*, 16.29, ll. 24–29.   [77] Paulos of Aigina, *Epitome*, 3.56.1.
[78] Translation in Ringrose, *Perfect Servant*, 54, slightly modified.
[79] E.g., Soranos, *Gynecology*, in Vilimonović, "Gender," 1210.

that sexual incompleteness was not always clear-cut that required the constant monitoring of the body to steer it aright – even if that required drastic interventions. To name one telling example, Paulos of Aigina offers detailed surgical instructions for removing enlarged mammary glands and adipose tissue from men (probably gynecomastia), "because the disgrace of having the unseemliness of femininity (θηλύτητα) is worthy of performing surgery (χειρουργεῖν ἄξιον)."[80] Judging from these texts, Grecophone Romans still largely operated within Aristotelian models of the malleable, androprimal body, where women were colder, men warmer, but both were still generally speaking on the same corporeal spectrum.[81]

Nor does it seem, judging from scholarship on later stages of Roman culture, that much had changed regarding views of the body. The work of Leonora Neville is especially relevant in this regard. Despite the fact that the bulk of the materials she studies come from the Makedonian and Komnenian eras, her findings show remarkable similarities to some of the key ideas just outlined. For instance, her analysis of later Roman evidence leads her to conclude that it is "reasonable to understand [Roman] masculinity as a matter of degree rather than an absolute attribute that one either has or has not."[82] She continues: "An adult male is a physiological ideal to which women, male and female children, and old men fell short."[83] In other words, there is no clear binary here, only sexed gradations. Neville's findings from a later era speak volumes about the remarkable continuity in Roman conceptions of sexual difference that were still largely consistent with the Aristotelian model of androprimacy.

We may attribute much of this consistency, perhaps, to persistent views of the body as intrinsically mutable.[84] If sex is determined by looking at the body, then it is impossible to achieve epistemological closure in virtue of the fickleness of the material substrate that composes it. The Confessor himself articulates this point unambiguously: "The alteration and mutability of the body and of external circumstances are for all humans one and the same thing – a carrying and a being carried along – and the only thing it has that can be called permanent and stable is its impermanence and instability."[85] The body was therefore a mutinous indicator of sex. As Judith Butler has famously argued, the determination of sex may be achieved through "the repeated stylization of the body, a set of repeated acts within a highly rigid regulatory frame that congeal over time to produce the appearance of substance, of a natural sort of being."[86] If so, Roman masculinity and its others might be better understood as a performative appearance preserved through an illusion of permanence impressed on the body, rather

---

[80] Paulos of Aigina, *Epitome*, 6.46.1.   [81] See further, Holmes, *Gender*, 37–45.
[82] Neville, *Byzantine Gender*, 26.   [83] Neville, *Byzantine Gender*, 26.
[84] See Holmes, *Gender*, 16.   [85] *Diff* 8.4.   [86] Butler, *Gender Trouble*, 33.

than as a stable essence rooted in an unchanging principle. This much is roughly consistent with Maximos' affirmation, covered in the introduction, that there exists no *logos* for masculinity or femininity; instead, these genders should be understood as modal inventions, not essential categories rooted in the divine *logoi*.

It also bears underlining that these models of sexual difference were not an abstraction for Maximos but the substance of his everyday life. If we reconsider some of his acquaintances in light of the foregoing considerations, it is apparent that he navigated a world of considerable sexual fluidity – likely without thinking much of it. For example, Maximos addressed the largest number of his known letters to Ioannes the *koubikoularios*, whose title insinuates his social status as a courtly eunuch. The Romans were not always sure of how to class eunuchs, as Ringrose explains: "Since eunuchs lacked sperm they, like women, also lacked heat. Although they might be considered men, eunuchs were imperfect men because of their sterility and cool temperature."[87] Alternatively, as an ascetic, the Confessor was aware that numerous opportunities for sanctified living existed beyond marriage and family-building, as he spent some five decades in a same-sex monastic partnership with Anastasios, much as his beloved teacher, Sophronios, spent nearly three decades with his monastic partner, Ioannes Moschos. Conversely, Maximos did not hesitate to emphasize or deemphasize the female status of his correspondents, depending on the context and the woman's self-stylization. As previously noted, Maximos impugned the *patrikia* Martina's involvement in the growing Monenergist controversy in virtue of her status as a woman.[88] By contrast, that patronizing attitude is entirely missing in his correspondence with the abbess Ioannia, whom he addresses with the same aplomb and self-abasing humility that he accords his male superiors, presumably owing to her status as a monastic leader.[89] I mention these examples from Maximos' life as a reminder that the sexual diversity I am pointing to constituted Maximos' quotidian environment and should not be jarring to modern readers – it certainly was not to him.

A piece in the puzzle is still missing, though, for in the Aristotelian model that we have overviewed, the body could be fluid to some degree, but never so much so that the female could become wholly male. And yet, I argue that the Confessor envisions the eschatological erasure of the female through sublimation into the male owing to his androprimal commitments. How is that possible if the Aristotelian framework disallows it? The following subsection addresses this question by introducing further changes in the conceptualization of sexual

---

[87] Ringrose, *Perfect Servant*, 53.　　[88] *Letter* 12, PG 91.461–464.

[89] For more on this, see Salés, "Maximos the Confessor's Correspondence" (forthcoming).

difference that occurred between classical antiquity and Maximos' time. After all, the Greek medical tradition based on Aristotle was not the only intellectual vector in the Confessor's ponderances on sexual difference, for his eschatology was also indebted to Paul's creative take on the so-called myth of the primal androgyne and on its Patristic reception.

The Myth of the Primal Androgyne

In 1974, Wayne Meeks published "The Image of the Androgyne,"[90] an influential article that reconfigured the study of sexual difference in late antiquity but not, ironically, in Maximian studies. I say "ironically" because Meeks begins this article with two quotes by Maximos that Jaroslav Pelikan had called to his attention.[91] In these quotes, both from *Thalassios* 48, Maximos recontextualizes the ostensible collapse of sexual difference hinted at in Gal 3:28 as a cosmically unifying moment effected by Christ. Meeks tantalizingly entertains the possibility that the Confessor literally means what he writes, but never returns to him.

The androgyne myth Meeks references posits a human originally unified in an androgynous, prelapsarian figure that became subsequently rent asunder into two sexes that crave their pretemporal wholeness. This interpretative phenomenon emerged in the later stages of Second Temple Judaism as a type of midrash on Gen 1–2 that later featured prominently in early Rabbinic and Christian literature.[92] While these midrashim were sometimes dependent on the Hellenistic culture that spread throughout the Mediterranean basin and eastward across the crumbling Achaemenid state following the campaigns of Alexandros the Great, at their core they remained centered on the Genesis creation story. So, while this figure may owe part of its existence to the eminently memorable speech of Aristophanes in Plato's *Symposium*, the image of the late ancient androgyne that Maximos inherited was also the yield of the hermeneutical husbandry of Jewish and Christian intellectuals cultivating the atavistic soil of the Genesis creation narratives with Hellenistic tools.

Partly owing to the determined Greek androprimacy already highlighted, some scholars routinely refer to this androgyne as a "male androgyne."[93] Dale Martin justifies this nomenclature by explaining that this figure amounts to little more than "the subsuming of the weaker female into the stronger male, the

---

[90] Meeks, "Image of the Androgyne," 165–208.

[91] Meeks, "The Image of the Androgyne," 165, n. 1.

[92] I discuss the Christian sources in the following sections. For some examples of Jewish literature on the subject, see *Bereshit Rabbah* 8:1 and *Berakhot* 61a:6–7.

[93] For an excellent overview of the androgyne imaginary in early Christianity, see Dunning, *Specters of Paul*, 7–10. See also Fatum, "Image of God," 56–137, especially 61–65; Boyarin, *Radical Jew*, 126; Martin, *Sex and the Single Savior*, 77–90.

masculinization of the female body, the supplying of male 'presence' (heat, for instance) for the former experience of female 'absence' (cold, understood as lack of fire)."[94] It is no coincidence that the image Martin paints of the androgyne bears a striking resemblance to the Aristotelian model of sexual difference already overviewed. And while it largely operates within those parameters, something has changed: The androgyne now appears capable of subsuming the female into himself through the impartation of a vital heat that is categorically foreclosed to the female body in classical Aristotelian physiology. This innovation to classical models made it possible for Christian eschatological hope to anticipate the erasure of the "imperfections" of bodies here below, which effectively meant the resolution of non-male bodies into a higher male state in the eternal hereafter. How did this development come about?

Alongside the medical and exegetical traditions just covered was an equally significant preoccupation with unity that can be traced to distinctive features of Platonic philosophy. Paul and Philo played a major role in combining and disseminating both aspects, which would go on to determine the interpretative framework of Maximos and his predecessors. These thinkers shared an intellectual saturation with the androgyny myth that was further inflected by what Benjamin Dunning calls "Platonic monism." In *Specters of Paul*, Dunning explores the varied instantiations of this idea in early Christian thought, particularly as it defined the conceptualization of sexed bodies situated midway between the Adam–Christ Pauline typology. Dunning offers the following exposition of the intersection of the androgyne myth with Platonic monism in relation to sexual difference:

> The dominant ideology of sexual difference in the Greco-Roman world was one that conceptualized this difference not in terms of an ontological and incommensurable binary, but rather on a single sliding scale fundamentally oriented toward maleness. The "myth of the primal androgyne" participated in this ideological formation in the writings of Philo and Paul ... the androgyny myth had a long reach, impinging on a broad swath of early Christian positions on the status and meaning of sexual difference. These were positions that shared a common eschatological goal: the eventual overcoming of anthropological differences through the triumph of unity "in Christ." Put another way, what we see in these various theologies is an entrenched and persistent preoccupation with the (always already) masculine One, a monistic orientation that was right at home in a broadly Platonic philosophical milieu.[95]

In his study, Dunning avoids Laqueur's grand-scale reductivism by exploring what he calls a "rough and tumble variety" of appropriations and transformations of the one-sex body in a range of early Christian sources and by

---

[94] Martin, *Sex and the Single Savior*, 84.　　[95] Dunning, *Specters of Paul*, 32.

highlighting the sources' own concerns and nuances.[96] Dunning's final product is a highly textured analysis that articulates localized differences among the sources while also anchoring their concerns in a logic of sexual monism that remains haunted by male discourse.

Accordingly, thinkers like Paul, Philo, Clement of Alexandria, and others examined by Dunning looked to an eschatological orientation toward unity in a oneness that is preemptively coded as masculine. In other words, the primal (and final) unity in the androgyne is already preconceived as a return to (androprimal) male singularity into which all sexual alterities are sublimated to dissolve multiplicity. Maximos should be understood as operating within the hermeneutical parameters of this exegetical legacy. The question in Maximos' case becomes one of continuity and change within the intellectual registers of the Greek medical tradition and the myth of the primal androgyne as exposited by these earlier authors. Unfortunately, very little has been penned on the subject in Maximos to help orient the discussion.

As a partial remedy, we can briefly consider a couple of literary genres that illustrate these gender tensions, namely the martyrologies and hagiographies of "unmen." Despite their otherwise predictable androcentrism, Christian martyrdoms frequently feature girls, boys, women, the elderly, and the enslaved, who frequently "unman" their Roman persecutors in the interest of demonstrating Christianity's superiority through a contestation of gender categories.[97] Significantly, while these texts subvert traditional Roman notions of masculinity, they ultimately supplant them with inventive forms of masculinity, that is, forms of Christian masculinity that are not themselves entirely detached from their cultural moorings.[98] These masculinities, in turn, are narratively postulated as normative and superior, and, tellingly, within the reach of young, old, enslaved, and female bodies through a dramatized performance in the arena that hinges on the martyr's self-stylization as a simulacrum of Christ.

A similar point can be made on the basis of transgender hagiographies. Recently, Roland Betancourt has called renewed attention to some three dozen such hagiographies written between the fifth and ninth century in the Roman Empire.[99] These hagiographies feature saints who were assigned female at birth but who subsequently – sometimes even by divine command, as in the case of Dorotheos of Egypt[100] – undergo extraordinary corporeal

---

[96] Dunning, *Specters of Paul*, 4.
[97] On this point, see Salés, "Queerly Christified Bodies," 83–109.
[98] See Gold, "And I Became a Man," 153–165; Cobb, *Dying to Be Men*, 33–59.
[99] See Betancourt, *Byzantine Intersectionality*, 89–120.
[100] This account survives in both Coptic and Greek and is known as the *Life of Apollinaria* or the *Life of Hilaria*.

transformations to masculinity by resorting to Greek medical knowledge and male-gendered dieting practices. Rather than censoring these saints for the temerity of becoming manly, their hagiographers praise them for their success in anticipating in this life the "perfect" (male) state of the afterlife. Indeed, the transgender saints themselves, if we can trust their hagiographers, commonly self-identified as male until death,[101] even when identifying as the sex they were assigned at birth would have spared them from slanderous ignominy.[102] Tellingly, no hagiographies exist praising the opposite (male→female) transition.

I find a few points about these two popular genres salient for late ancient Christian notions of the sexed body in relation to Maximos. First, the "natural" sex of martyrs is only underlined by the authors as a means of showing that even that aspect of their identity did not hinder their attainment of an idealized form of Christian masculinity. In fact, many martyrdoms actively erase martyr's female features, such as when Perpetua rejects her motherhood and her breasts miraculously cease lactating during her imprisonment or when she usurps the gladiator's phallic privilege by plunging his blade into herself.[103] Conversely, authors might underline the martyr's catachrestic masculinity through subversions of social expectations, such as when Blandina exhausts her tormentors by being able to take more pain than they can inflict or when she appears before her brethren as Christ crucified for them.[104] More gruesome martyrdoms even dwell on the mutilation of martyr's breasts, as in the cases of Febronia of Nisibis and Anahid of Persia.[105] Conversely, transgender saints can effect substantive changes on the body previously coded as female – and unlike the classical tale of Phaethousa, the result is not death but holiness described in male terms. Indeed, the attainment of monastic perfection for transgender saints is often expressed in gendered physical terms that elide female secondary characteristics. For example, some authors go out of their way to praise formerly female saints for succeeding in shriveling their breasts into nonexistence, for becoming "dried up" and warm (quintessentially male attributes in Aristotelian medicine), or for achieving premature menopause.[106]

---

[101] E.g., Pelagia/Pelagios of Antioch and Maria/Marinos.

[102] E.g., Marinos in relation to the charge of impregnating an inn-keeper's daughter. For an English translation, see Talbot, ed., *Holy Women of Byzantium*, 1–12. For further discussion, see Davis, "Crossed Texts, Crossed Sex," 1–36.

[103] *Passion of Perpetua* 6, 21 (respectively), ed. Heffernan.

[104] Eusebios of Kaisareia, *Ecclesiastical History*, 5.1.18–19.

[105] For Anahid, see Bedjan, *Acta martyrum et sanctorum*, vol. 2, 565–603. For Febronia, see Bedjan, *Acta martyrum et sanctorum*, vol. 5, 573–615. For English translations of the Syriac, see Brock and Harvey, trans., *Holy Women of the Syrian Orient*, 82–99 (Anahid) and 152–176 (Febronia).

[106] *Acta S. Pelagiae Syriace*, ed. Gildmeister, and *Vita Mariae Aegyptiacae*, PG 87.3:3697A–3726D. For English translations, see Brock and Harvey, trans., *Holy Women*, 40–62 (Pelagia/Pelagios) and Talbot, ed., *Holy Women of Byzantium*, 65–93 (Maria).

My point in bringing up these bodies of literature is to show the pervasiveness of the model of sexual dynamism that permeated the Confessor's culture in a literary register different than speculative, dogmatic, theological, or medical thought. This literature shows how broadly diffused these views of the sexed body were. Further, what was particularly outstanding about Christian theorizing about the body was that masculinity no longer remained categorically foreclosed to all who were not assigned male at birth, at least in some ways. Hence Gregory of Nyssa's famed tribute to his sister Makrina: "And the subject of the narrative was a woman – if indeed a woman, for I do not know whether it is suitable to designate her by her nature who came to be higher than her nature."[107] Makrina's sanctity elevates her past womanhood. The highest level of holiness virtually demanded the stylized transformation of the body – however assigned at birth – into a visible foretaste of the ostensibly sexless eschatological body, even if that transfigured body remained suspiciously male.

In this sense, then, Christianity had flipped the classical script: While in the Aristotelian tradition it was the male who could "backslide" into femininity, in some early Christian thought it was now the female who could attain an idealized masculinity – even if only partially in this life. Sanctity was unidirectionally manward. No saint is commemorated for having transitioned into femininity, in large part because in the early Christian androprimal imagination, the female was considered an evanescent detour of uncertain ontological status midway between Adam's primacy and Christ's finality. So, if the female body represented a metaphysical "problem," it was one that could be relegated to the eschatological resolution of difference partially anticipated by the metamorphosis to which it could be subjected in this life through asceticism. In the end, as in the beginning, there could only be the male, and that outcome was the effect of Greco-Roman Christian androprimacy.

Conclusion

When viewed together, the diverse traditions on the body and sexual difference we have examined in this section yield a clearer picture of Greco-Roman Christian androprimacy and the ideologies that sustained it. These ideologies stemmed from the coalescence of the Aristotelian-Platonic and biblical traditions concerning human origins and the grounds of sexual difference. In this account, the male was seen as both the first human and thus as generic for the species: androprimacy grounded andronormativity and, of course, the sociopolitical structures predicated on these assumptions. But Christian soteriology further anticipated the eschatological unity brought about by Christ that could

---

[107] *Life of Saint Makrina* 1, ll. 14–17, ed. Maraval.

be partly achieved in this life. This unity did not preserve the sexual specificity of embodied individuals in this life, nor did it presage an end to sex as such. Rather, the end in view presupposed a male singularity as the pinnacle of human existence that was foreshadowed by Adam and fulfilled by Christ.

As such, later Christian receptions of Paul's message of Christian universality devoid of anthropological differentials (Gal 3:28) were bound to stand in tension with his Adam–Christ typology (Rom 5:12–21), which featured two male-sexed individuals as beginning and consummation of the human species. Androprimacy therefore must look to female sublimation to restore this primordial order. This outcome was predictable given Christian attempts to address the aforementioned Pauline tension by resorting to a Greek ideological apparatus inescapably beset by sexist presuppositions. Of course, amid these intellectualized discussions we should not lose sight of the fact that androprimacy is the abstract name for a harmful social force whose effects were (and are) painfully real. Romans regarded sexual alterities (to the male) as a faint and unstable reiteration, a derivative second, and an (un)original "other" that failed to realize the male ideal situated at the top of an ontologically hierarchized pyramid. In this framework, non-males could approximate perfection not in their own right and along a separate axis but by conforming in this life to an idealized male they asymptotically became by the quotidian abnegation of their being.[108]

2 A New Reading of *Difficulty* 41

This section investigates the subtle convergence of Greco-Roman Christian androprimacy and the myth of the male androgyne in *Difficulty* 41, Maximos' classical text on sexual difference. Specifically, these two traditions intersect in the figure of Christ, who consummates the nature of the "human" (ἄνθρωπος/ *anthropos*) because he overcomes sexual difference where Adam failed. However, in treating both the "human" (implicitly the fallen male androgyne or Adam) and Christ (the male androgyne as he should have been) as male-sexed beings, Maximos undercuts a consistent sexless anthropology. Instead, the human remains a male singularity typified by Adam and fulfilled by Christ that renders female subjectivity contingent and uncertain. What is certain is that the erasure of masculinity as such was never in the cards. For this reason, I always translate "human" with male forms, in keeping with Greek. In so doing, I also wish to highlight further the casual pervasiveness of Maximos' androprimal assumptions.

---

[108] For a short list of orienting studies on Roman gender, see Neville, *Byzantine Gender*, 5–22, 33–58; Andreou, "'Emotioning' Gender," 35–63; Rosser, *Women, Science, and Myth*, 3–30; Nifosi, *Becoming a Woman*, 13–48; Kuefler, *Manly Eunuch*, 19–36.

In the broadest sense, *Difficulty* 41 is an apologetic for and expansion on Gregory of Nazianzos' seemingly innocuous statement that "natures are innovated and God becomes a human" that allows Maximos to paint an elaborate picture of his vision for cosmic unity in Christ. The *Difficulty* is especially concerned with clarifying how this innovation does not change what nature is but how it subsists. That is, nature only changes in its mode of existence; its defining limits remain unaltered.

At *Difficulty* 41.2, Maximos introduces his now famed fivefold division of the "subsistence of realities that have come into being" (τὴν πάντων τῶν γεγονότων ὑπόστασιν):

1 uncreated nature/created nature
2 intelligible nature/sensible nature
3 heaven/earth
4 paradise/inhabited world
5 male/female

If examined closely, these divisions are linked to one another, except for the last, as Dewhurst has noted.[109] That is, the second through fourth divisions are a subset of a higher division: Created nature is divided into intelligible and sensible nature, sensible nature into heaven and earth, and earth into paradise and the inhabited world. The fifth division does not follow this sequence, as only human nature, and not the entire inhabited world, is split into male and female. I will comment on this point later, when discussing 41.9.

But what of the first division? Of what is it a division? At first, Maximos calls it "the subsistence of all realities that have come into being" (τὴν πάντων τῶν γεγονότων ὑπόστασιν). But γεγονότων fits ill with the "uncreated," as the uncreated is not typically considered to "have come into being." Is it possible that Maximos departs from this language next by dividing the two categories under the larger term of "nature" (φύσις)? If so, the first division would seem to be of "nature" rather than "the subsistence of all realities that have come into being," as he clarifies in the next phrase, where he refers to created nature specifically as "receiving its being through origination (διὰ γενέσεως τὸ εἶναι λαβοῦσαν),"[110] unlike uncreated nature. But the tension cannot be eased so easily because both terms are still subject to the term "nature" and thus remain ontologically commensurable in some way. What is at issue here?

Maximos is likely implying the distinction between *logos* and *tropos*, whereby beings can be understood from two simultaneously predicated criteria, predicated, however, in different regards. All beings are constituted by created

---

[109] Dewhurst, "Absence of Sexual Difference," 205.   [110] *Diff* 41.2.

and uncreated dimensions: The divine blueprint of each being is uncreated, that to which it gives concrete existence is created. A clearer exposition of this distinction appears in *Chapters on Theology* 1.48, where Maximos distinguishes between "God's works" that begin temporally and those that do not. The former refer to "all participating beings, such as the different substances of beings, since they have non-being prior to their existence," while the latter refer to "participated realities, in which participating beings participate by grace, such as goodness and anything particular that is encompassed by the principle of goodness."[111] So, "the uncreated" refers to that which is predicated of God absolutely and of humans qualifiedly (e.g., goodness, existence, beauty); the created refers to concrete beings (e.g., Metrodora, Secretariat, Maximos) who come into existence by the confluence of these uncreated features.[112] Put another way, the uncreated aspects of beings constitute nature in aggregate form as its definition, while the created aspects of beings are subject to space, time, change, and invention.[113] This distinction matters because on it hinges whether terms such as "male" or "female" are uncreated or created, that is, whether they are natural or contrived. Significantly, *Difficulty* 41 treats sexual difference as the latter.[114]

After these preliminary schematics, Maximos next lays out the original plan for the human to cosmically unite nature by "fulfilling" (συμπληρούμενος) the divine plan in himself. At 41.2, Maximos maintains that the first human's purpose was to unify the divisions through his "potential for unity" (τὴν πρὸς ἕνωσιν δύναμιν), to "render manifest in himself the great mystery of the divine intention when he had harmoniously completed in full the reciprocal union in God of the extremes that are in beings, proceeding upward sequentially from the proximate to the distant and from the lesser to the greater."[115] When Maximos says, "from the proximate to the distant," he means the encompassing range of each division, from the most universal (uncreated/created) to the least universal (male/female).[116] But when he adds "from the lesser to the greater," is it not obvious that for him each tier is hierarchical? Maximos surely means that uncreated nature is greater than created nature (first division), intelligible than sensible (second division), heaven than earth (third division), paradise than inhabited world (fourth division) – and we can see where he is going in the fifth division. Additionally, an analogous structure of androprimacy is also appreciable in the other four divisions, where the "lesser" cosmic divisions have a history of being coded as female, the "greater" as male (see Section 3).

---

[111] *ChTh* 1.48.   [112] A comparable example can be found in *Diff* 7.21–22.
[113] For background and elucidation, see Tollefsen, *Christocentric Cosmology*, 27–63.
[114] See Dewhurst, "Absence of Sexual Difference," 206–207.   [115] *Diff* 41.2.
[116] See further, Cvetković, "Logoi," 81–93.

After explaining how the upward unifying sequence works, Maximos next spells out the human's unifying potential after he reaches the limit of the highest ascent in God by

> altogether shaking off from nature, by the most dispassionate constitution in relation to divine virtue, the characteristic of female and of male (which was obviously in no way bound to the original *logos* of the divine intention concerning the origin of the human) in order to be both apprehended as and become simply a human, not being divided by the term corresponding to "male" and "female" (κατὰ τὸ ἄρσεν καὶ τὸ θῆλυ προσηγορίᾳ); indeed, according to that *logos* [of human], he had originally come into being without being mutilated into the pieces now around him (τοῖς νῦν περὶ αὐτὸν οὖσι τμήμασι μὴ μεριζόμενον), owing to the perfect union to his own *logos*, as I said, according to which he exists.[117]

This passage indicates that virtue is responsible for "shaking off" from nature through dispassion the "characteristic" (ἰδιότης) of female and male – as if they were ontologically tumorous. Let's be clear: The object of eradication here is not the division but the *characteristic* of male and female undergirding the division. Granted, the emphasis on virtue here might lend some credence to Thunberg's psychologizing thesis, but on the whole, this passage cannot support that interpretation. For one, Maximos regularly refers to the virtues of the body along with the virtues of the soul,[118] and it is precisely many of these virtues of the body (fasting, vigilance, endurance, etc.) that often resignify the sexing of the saintly body. This point is at work here too, as Maximos affirms that the virtues have direct bearing on the characteristic (ἰδιότης) of sexual difference. Most significantly, the Confessor insists these characteristics "obviously" (δηλαδή) have no *logos* in nature and are therefore inconsistent with the divine intention. Another problem with the psychologizing interpretation is that Maximos never argues that desire and drive must be eliminated from the soul, only that they should be subordinated to reason.[119] Because drive and desire are constitutive of the soul, thus of nature, their eradication would corrupt nature.[120] The same cannot be said about male and female, as no *logos* essentially anchors them.[121] Simply, sexual difference can be erased without corrupting nature.

---

[117] *Diff* 41.3.
[118] For the relation of virtue, body, and passions, see *ChL* 1.76, 2.57; *ChTh* 1.80, 2.79, 2.88.
[119] See further, e.g., *Diff* 48, as well as Larchet, *La divinisation*, 128–129.
[120] Compare with how Maximos explains Gregory of Nyssa's affirmations surrounding the emotions in *Thal* 1. See also Gregory of Nyssa, *On the Soul and the Resurrection*, 35–36, ed. Spira. On the emotions and psychological capacities in Gregory more generally, see Salés, "'Can These Bones Live?'" 44–50. Relatedly, Blowers, *Maximus*, 258–279 and the earlier article on the same subject, "Dialectics and Therapeutics," 425–451.
[121] As Dewhurst rightly notes in "Absence of Sexual Difference," 206.

Tellingly, this erasure begins with the female. Although Greek style over-whelmingly favors syntactical androprimacy, Maximos writes that the supremely dispassionate human shakes off from nature "the characteristic of *female* and of male." Presumably, Maximos catachrestically places female first because she vanishes first following the sequence from the "lesser to the greater" (41.2). The male nowhere seems any more evanescent than uncreated or intelligible nature. Indeed, Maximos repeats a similar process in 41.7 by hypothetically vacating gendered space only for androprimacy to reinscribe itself on it. So, after noting in 41.4–6 how the first human could have bridged all five divisions, the Confessor next explains how Christ succeeded in exiling male–female division and difference to the proverbial hinterlands of ontological superfluity:

> Beginning the universal union of all realities to Himself on the basis of our division, [Christ] becomes a perfect human, having without deficiency from us, for us, consistent with us all that is ours, "save sin,"[122] (because, to this end, He stood in no need of the consequence of marriage consummation as in nature) – actually, come to think of it, He has shown by this very fact that perhaps there was another mode as well, foreknown to God, for the propaga-tion of humans into a multitude (εἰς πλῆθος τῶν ἀνθρώπων αὐξήσεως) if the first human had observed the commandment and if he had not cast himself down to animality (κτηνωδίαν) by a mode that misuses (παράχρησιν τρόπῳ) his own capacities – and banishing the difference and division corresponding to male and female, of which He stood in no need, as I said, to have become a human, and without which it is perhaps possible to exist. There is no need for these to endure in perpetuity, "for in Christ Jesus," the divine apostle says, "[there is] neither male nor female (Gal 3:28)."[123]

Here, Christ unifies all humans, without leaving anything natural behind, under a single human umbrella presumably transcending sexual difference. The con-text here is concerned with the eradication of the division and difference of sexed bodies that Christ accomplishes by the unsexing resignification of his own body.

In this last regard, 41.7 introduces a further layer to the discussion by adding sexual difference, not just division, to the mix. This addition matters because differences refer to qualities by which individual entities are categorized into larger groups that simultaneously differentiate them from others.[124] Here,

---

[122] Heb 4:15.

[123] *Diff* 41.7. This passage shares some similarities with Gregory of Nyssa's *On the Making of the Human* 17.2.

[124] For more details on the philosophical background, see Cvetković, "Logoi," 194–200; Erismann, "Logician for East and West," 50–68; and especially Tollefsen, *Christocentric Cosmology*, 100–101.

Maximos seems to be concerned with sexual reproduction and the risk it poses to human differentiation from animals. Otherwise, how to explain his latent concern that the sundering of humanity into sexual alterities for the sake of animalistic heterosexual reproduction misuses human capacities? Indeed, heterosexual intercourse and its unnatural corporeal preconditions appear to be, themselves, somehow linked to the ancestral sin.[125] If so, and since there is no *logos* of sexual specificity (i.e., male or female), Maximos reasonably concludes that "there is no need for these to endure in perpetuity," as they are inconsistent with both the divine intention and the embodiment of human perfection accomplished by Christ. Hence, Maximos emphasizes that these differentiations are unnatural and have no ontological foundation, even if, as in 41.3, the figure transcending sexual difference is male. Ironically, herein also lies a moment of constructive opportunity. While prima facie Maximos treats Christ as male, the text is ambiguous about his sexual status. In arguing for Christ's eradication of sexual difference, the Confessor claims twice that sexual difference was not necessary for Christ to become a human. Does he mean that sexual difference was unnecessary insofar as Christ was conceived without a heterosexual reproductive encounter or that Christ as such was neither male nor female? I will return to the second alternative in the conclusion of this Element.

On the first option, if sexual differentiation is a result of sin, or at least implicated with sin, Christ's incarnation must bypass that reproductive system by "innovating nature." To this end, Maximos reasons that Christ can assume human nature whole without needing to be the "consequence of marriage consummation." Maximos' bashful monastic euphemism for sex suggests that the fullness of Christ's humanity is independent of the reproductive biomechanics of his conception. Christ need not be born heterosexually to be fully human – parthenogenesis will do just fine.[126] But why is heterosexual reproduction itself a problem? For one, it sunders humans into sexual alterities and requires what Maximos in no uncertain terms calls a misuse of the human capacities. Similarly, how would Christ overcome heterosexuality and sexual difference if he is the direct result of, and also furthers, both in his own person? Another problem might be that sin could be transmitted through the seed, as if a sexually transmitted hamartiological infection à la Augustine.[127] And yet, Maximos seems unconcerned that Mary could transmit sin to Christ, which suggests that he regards the male seed as implicated with the transmission of sin, while the maternal body, following Aristotle, is solely the purveyor of matter.

---

[125] See Dewhurst, "Absence of Sexual Difference," 205.

[126] See Sonea, "Man's Mission," 181–185.

[127] See Larchet, *La divinisation*, 206–207, and relatedly, Berthold, "Did Maximus the Confessor Know Augustine?" 14–17.

Maximos' focus on sexed bodies and reproduction may be easier to tease out by simplifying the syntax of 41.7. This text is made up of a main clause split by both an anacoluthon and a parenthetical aside expressed as a genitive absolute. The anacoluthon is an interruption of the Confessor's thought process meant to address an implied objection to his suggestion that humans could exist as non-sexed beings. The objection would interrogate humanity's reproductive outlook in such a scenario, and the anacoluthon is meant to ease the anxiety motivating the objection. The main clause thus argues that humans are modally, not naturally, sexed; if so, sexual difference corresponds to nothing proper to the human *logos* (as affirmed in 41.3), representing instead an arbitrary mode of existence devoid of metaphysically anchoring content. That is why the Confessor's final phrase in the governing clause is no longer concerned with reproduction, which the anacoluthon ostensibly addressed, but with the possibility that humans might be able to exist (εἶναι) without sexual differentiation. The outcome is pyrrhic. The subtextual saturation of this passage in androprimal discourse can and should be pointed out for the ways in which it ultimately constrains the Confessor's success in postulating a human being that eludes the discourse of androprimacy as much as for how it reinforces female occlusion. However, we should remain cognizant that Maximos was also a seventh-century Roman monk who undertook an ambitious project to conceptualize human singularity without sexual difference in favor of a universality portended by a Christian savior of a potentially uncertain sexual identity. The promise, if not the execution, of this latter point should not be lightly overlooked.

The Confessor continues pondering eschatological sexlessness in Christ in 41.9, where he offers some concluding remarks on Christ's alleged eradication of male and female:

> Having united us to ourselves in Himself, first through the removal of the difference of male and female, He proved [that we are] – instead of men and women, in whom the mode of the division is especially observed – properly and truly simply humans, wholly configured after Him, bearing His image undiminished and entirely unalloyed, tampered with in no way whatsoever by any of the telltale signs of corruption.[128]

As in 41.7, Maximos not only emphasizes Christ's removal of the difference,[129] not only the division, between male and female, but adds several significant points.[130] For example, the Confessor's reference to "men and women" implies that he is

---

[128] *Diff* 41.9.

[129] For the significance of this kind of difference, see *Diff* 22, as well as Tollefsen, *Christocentric Cosmology*, 98–99.

[130] Agreeing here with Mitralexis, "Rethinking the Problem of Sexual Difference," 139–144.

speaking of sexed human bodies with reproductive capabilities.[131] Similarly, Maximos qualifies "men and women" – not just "male and female" – as something belonging to the *mode* of human existence that corrupts God's handiwork. Even the rhetorical syntax of this passage, "instead of men and women" (ἀντὶ ἀνδρῶν καὶ γυναικῶν), indicates that he wishes to cross out sexual difference before he even names it, seeing in it a tragically defining feature (γνώρισμα) of the ancestral forgery that stamped it upon every subsequent human image of God.

Finally, in the anacoluthon above, Maximos notes that Christ demonstrates that we are not "men and women, in whom the mode of the division is especially observed." We may ask "especially observed" in comparison to what or whom? If we recall, in 41.2, Maximos does not preserve a strict correspondence between the fourth and the fifth divisions. Between the fourth and fifth division, Maximos had made a change, where it is human nature, not the inhabited world, that is divided into male and female.[132] I would venture to guess that Maximos is contrasting humans with the other inhabitants of the world, animals and plants, who make no such distinction among themselves and whose sex is often harder to discern than that of humans. He may possibly also mean that the division into male and female is seen most clearly in the case of men and women in contradistinction to other humans who elude this binary: children and early youths, certainly,[133] but probably also eunuchs and the elderly – or even ascetics, whose sex is not always self-evident (e.g., the famous first encounter between Maria of Egypt and Zosimas).

Further evidence for why Maximos cannot envision the perpetuity of sexual difference appears in a passage that is rarely consulted in relation to this subject.[134] At 41.10, Maximos outlines a taxonomy heavily reliant on the divisions of nature in Aristotle's *Categories* later refined in Porphyrios' *Eisagoge*. This taxonomy is made up of genus, species, individual, and accident. Each of these has unity by more generic principles. So, a genus is constituted by many species when their differentiations are removed and a species is constituted by many individuals when their differentiations are removed, whereas individuals are constituted by their accidents. This much is implicit when Maximos claims that "all realities individually distinguished from one another by their own differences are generically unified by universal and common identities, and are reciprocally driven toward one and the same by a certain generic *logos* of nature."[135] That is to say that as we bracket away the

---

[131] See further Dewhurst, "Absence of Sexual Difference," 209.
[132] Dewhurst rightly identifies this subtle change: "Absence of Sexual Difference," 205.
[133] See Salés, "Queerly Christified Bodies," 100.
[134] Dewhurst is the exception in this regard. See Dewhurst, "Absence of Sexual Difference," 208.
[135] *Diff* 41.10.

differences by which species are constituted by their otherness from other species, they are all subsumed under a larger, more comprehensive genus. Dogs and dolphins seem different enough unless we see them as mammals.

The same logic applies as we descend downward in this ontological arrangement. The lowest level of differentiation is that of the individual, constituted by a conglomerate of accidents (συμβεβηκότα). These accidents together yield concrete individuals.[136] What is especially surprising of this essential being is that each is defined by a unique *logos*, as Torstein Tollefsen underlines: "Maximus actually teaches the existence of essences of *particulars* with *logoi* of their own."[137] There is thus a *logos* of each individual being, and not just of a species. Accordingly, material accidents are not the sole reason for individuated existence, as in Aristotelian metaphysics, but also a divine rationale or *logos* underlying every being. Therefore, individuals constitute entire species when aggregated, but species without individuals, as much as genera without species, do not exist. Maximos famously makes this point in *Difficulty* 10.101, by noting that if individuals or particulars were destroyed, so too would be the universals comprised by them. But the opposite is not the case: Species and genera have no separable existence from the individuals who constitute them.

These metaphysical disquisitions matter because they preclude any taxonomy of sexual difference. Difference (διαφορά) designates simultaneously a similarity within a group that differentiates it from another group in order to constitute a separate species or genus,[138] as Tollefsen lucidly explains: "As constitutive or essential, the differences are contemplated with a view to the community they establish between beings of the same species ... Seen in this way, differences are mainly understood as collective or inclusive."[139] Thus, there cannot be a *logos* of male and female to ontologically fix sexual difference, understood as a differentiating principle, because doing so would mean that "male" and "female" designate different species, a conclusion that would yield myriad absurdities. If any of the terms of sexual difference were a universal, the term would have to designate a species through the constitution of an essentializing differentiation (εἰδοποιὸς διαφορά), but male and female are not the type of differences that constitute varied species.[140] Such an argument would directly contradict the Confessor's earlier statements on the matter

---

[136] Compare with Tollefsen, *Christocentric Cosmology*, 85.

[137] Tollefsen, *Christocentric Cosmology*, 85.

[138] Compare, on these points, with Aristotle, *Metaphysics,* 10.9, and *Politics*, 1260a12–13.

[139] Tollefsen, *Christocentric Cosmology*, 100.

[140] For an excellent discussion of the underlying Aristotelian and Porphyrian logic here, see Tollefsen, *Christocentric Cosmology*, 98–99.

at 41.3, where he rejects the existence of a *logos* that differentiates human nature sexually. Simply, no *logos* of "male" or "female" exists.

The only possibility left to consider is to attribute sexual difference to the level of accidents in the material substrate. The result of this solution is not sexual binarity, though, but sexual specificities arranged, as we saw in Section 1, along a vertical axis oriented toward masculinity (at least in Maximos' context). In this scenario, because unity of accidents can only be found at the level of the individual and not, one taxonomic level higher, at the level of species, sexual specificity becomes individuated and unified solely at the individual level. At this point, it would be helpful to recollect that Aristotle had maintained in *Metaphysics* 10 that men and women do not constitute different species, since they have no essential differences. Maximos similarly seems to conceptualize unified human nature as a species that shares ontological continuity and that cannot be divided into "sexual species" (such as male or female), solely because of material differences.

Conclusion

This section offered a new reading of *Difficulty* 41 through the lens of Greco-Roman Christian androprimacy and foregrounded the various hints in this text that signal the Confessor's tacit understanding that the female body is destined for eschatological sublimation into the male. This much is apparent in the hierarchy of the five divisions (41.2); the last division, that into male and female, identifies the female as "lesser" and the male as "greater." At the same time, Maximos also seems to intimate that the male as such is also eschatologically overcome, and that that process is already somehow fulfilled in Christ. But there is the rub: The Confessor wants simultaneously to posit existence beyond sexual difference without relinquishing the most basic structure of androprimal discourse. Accordingly, the first human, Adam, and the final human, Christ, are both male-coded – Maximos certainly treats them as such. Therefore, when he speculates that it might be possible for humans to exist without sexual difference, that prospect must be understood in the context of a totalizing male protology and eschatology that finds universality in the idealized male form of the human being. Accordingly, non-males fit ill at either end of the chronological register. This hermeneutical insecurity with the female in particular is readily apparent elsewhere, especially in texts where the Confessor chiastically envelopes and ultimately elides Eve and Mary within the male metonymy of Adam and Christ, as the following section shows.

3 Eve and Mary in Maximos' Exegesis

The Confessor's discussion of sexual difference in *Difficulty* 41 is abstract in that Christ is the only named protagonist and the backdrop is nebulously defined. By contrast, this section explores Maximos' concrete exposition of Adam, Eve, Mary, and Christ in texts that feature specific problematics and well-defined parameters that further exhibit Maximos' tacit commitments to androprimacy. As in *Difficulty* 41, androprimacy remains the prism through which the ascetic author's hermeneutical vision is refracted and leads him to deploy strategies of figurative displacement, discursive erasure, and objectifying materialization of Eve and Mary. In this, Maximos is part of a long-standing Patristic tradition of expositing a Pauline theological anthropology that struggled with the proto-logical and eschatological placement of both women – and of all by extension.

In the following texts, androprimacy exerts a logically destabilizing force on Maximos' reasoning, particularly when it pushes him to retrench positions he sought to bypass. That is especially true when he discusses desire and reproduction, where Eve and Mary play vital, but ultimately devalued and insufficient, roles in the narrative arc of fall and restoration. Maximos often hesitates to identify Eve in a creation sequence that foregrounds the "forefather" (i.e., Adam) while maintaining his idiosyncratic belief that the fall – and with it sexual difference – happened at the exact moment that the human came into being. Similarly, while explicating Mary's role in redemption, the Confessor unsuccessfully attempts to elude the reproductive economy set in motion by the fall by displacing the role that seed plays in embryonal gestation, only to then attribute it to Christ as the principle of his own gestation. In brief, Maximos' exegesis throughout presupposes the categorical insufficiency of both women, so that in a pattern reminiscent of *Difficulty* 41, they, too, are variously sublimated by their male counterparts. Still, Maximos is ultimately unable to eradicate the female or positively to articulate a human universality – even a monadic male humanity – that does not somehow presuppose the very alterities and oppositions it pretends to erase. If some of these contradictions seem familiar, it is because they are Christianized echoes of Aristotle's sexually differentiated anthropology.

Eve

Compared to earlier Grecophone Christians, Maximos' references to Eve are notably sparse and cursory, referring to her by name no more than a handful of times in his entire corpus and in most instances because the underlying passage he is exegeting obliges him.[141] Eve's evanescent quality in Maximos' reflections on

---

[141] E.g., *QDoub* 1.3.

Eden is unusual if we consider that she was predominantly the subject of appalling misogynistic ire in the Patristic era for allegedly precipitating humanity's downfall. And while Maximos does belchingly join that cacophonous choir on a pair of occasions,[142] he rarely implicates her in the fall in a crassly literalistic way.

Some have interpreted Eve's seeming absence in Maximos' sketch of the atavistic lapse positively, taking it as indication of Adam's central, perhaps sole, culpability.[143] However, I find this interpretation unhelpful and ethically counterproductive. For one, commitment to feminist liberation today should not be procedurally predicated (even if at times it regrettably, though not entirely inexplicably, has been) on turning the tables of patriarchal power dynamics back on men. Further, I fail to see how erasing women from the mythohistorical record – however fraught their representation within it might be – amounts to a sustainable anti-misogynistic intervention. But more to the point of this section, this interpretation misses a troubling exegetical manipulation of the symbolic economy whereby Eve *is* in fact at the center of the protological indiscretion.

The bulk of the Confessor's exegeses of the paradisiacal debacle represent inventive adaptations of long-standing hermeneutical predilections especially reminiscent of Clement of Alexandria and others whose interpretative lineaments were traced within the boundaries of the myth of the primal androgyne. In these traditions, Eve is also sometimes hard to find as a concrete individual, but she is not, for that, somehow absolved of guilt or absent from setting the transgression in motion. Rather, in these earlier and quite sophisticated Patristic accounts, Eve is often displaced by pleasure or desire, or is often protologically subsumed under the unified figure of Adam/the androgyne as the forefather of all humanity. A strikingly similar pattern emerges in the Confessor's own explication of the anthropological rupture that took place in Eden.

Part of my hermeneutical angle here is indebted to Benjamin Dunning's shrewd reading of several early Christian interpreters of the status of Eve and Mary, especially Irenaios and Clement. Dunning attributes the exegetical strategy of Eve's displacement in Clement's *Protreptikos* to the various ways in which the Pauline Adam–Christ typology, in which neither Eve nor Mary can ultimately have a permanent place, requires the occlusion of the female for the appearance of androcentric unity and the narrative integrity of the typology.[144] Thus, Eve can be replaced by desire or pleasure, so that the motivating force that caused Adam's transgression remains in play while simultaneously ironing out the wrinkles in the Pauline typology by sequestering her into hypostatic

---

[142] E.g., *Diff* 7.32; *QDoub* 1.3.   [143] E.g., Costache, "Living Above Gender," 267.
[144] Dunning, *Specters of Paul*, 57.

invisibility. In Dunning's words: "Thus, while neither Eve nor the feminine is mentioned in the creation narrative of *Protrepticus* II, two other concepts (characters?) fill the gap in the story: pleasure (*hēdonē*) and desire (*epithymiais*). In this account of the garden, the first human falls victim to pleasure and is led astray by desire."[145] A similar process is seemingly afoot in the Confessor's exegesis of Eden, albeit nuanced further by subsequent developments in Patristic exegeses of Gen 1–3.

Specifically, Maximos rethought, and incorporated into his exegesis, certain aspects of Gregory of Nyssa's protology. Andrew Louth has noticed this connection, underlining how Maximos critically redeploys Gregory's so-called "double creation" theory.[146] This theory refers to Gregory's belief that God intended for humans to reproduce up to a predetermined number in an angel-like manner, while simultaneously, in anticipation of the human transgression that would thwart them from reaching that number, God equipped humans with an animalistic failsafe mechanism for continuing reproduction through physical procreation.[147] As some have pointed out,[148] Gregory's theory runs aground when he affirms that the body liable to passions given in anticipation of the fall becomes itself the cause of the fall – how, in other words, does it make sense for God to make a postlapsarian mitigating factor the very motor that precipitates a transgression that would never happen without it?[149]

Instead, Maximos postulates a highly idiosyncratic and largely unprecedented take: He accepts Gregory's speculation about human nonsexual reproduction and the interrelationship of sex and the transgression, but nowhere holds that humans received a pre-sexed body in anticipation of the fall, that this body precipitated it, or that its purpose was to attain a predetermined number of humans thereafter. Rather, and quite strikingly, Maximos affirms the simultaneity of human origins, sexual difference, and the fall.[150] As such, the sexed and fallen body have never been spatiotemporally separable – only the *logos* of humanity can be postulated as logically prior, but that *logos* is sexless. Thus, identifying Eve in Maximos' exegesis requires a hermeneutic attuned to dynamic modes of resignifying strategies that, like those of Clement and Gregory, are rarely discursively transparent.

---

[145] Dunning, *Specters of Paul*, 58.

[146] Louth, *Maximus*, 156; Garrigues, *Maxime le Confesseur*, 178.

[147] *On the Nature of the Human*, 17.3–4.

[148] See Szczerba, "Podwójne stworzenie," 91–101; Marunová, "Nourishment in Paradise," 55–63; Zachhuber, *Human Nature*, 163–174; Ludlow, *Universal Salvation*, 45–76.

[149] *On the Nature of the Human* 18.3–5. See also *On the Soul and the Resurrection*, 14.7–8. See also Salés, "Can These Bones Live?," 58.

[150] See Blowers, "Gentiles of the Soul," 57–85.

Questions and Doubts *1.3*

This text is Maximos' most straightforward on Eve's role in the fall. Here, Maximos portrays her in a pattern reminiscent of Clement's *Protreptikos* 2, but with a catch. Maximos' response is a nearly verbatim quote that he approvingly cites from Athanasios of Alexandria's *Commentary on the Psalms*,[151] which associates Eve with pleasure, but without entirely removing her from the picture. This is how Athanasios/Maximos exegetes Ps 51:7 (LXX, "I was conceived in iniquity and in sins my mother bore me"):

> Since the primordial intention of God was for us not to be born through sex and corruption – but the transgression of the commandment introduced sex due to Adam's lawlessness, that is, by rejecting the law given him by God – therefore all who are born from Adam are *conceived in iniquity*, falling under the forefather's sentence. Conversely, *and in sins my mother bore me* means that Eve, the mother of us all, first bore sin when she was in heat for pleasure. For this reason, we say that we too are born in sins, falling under the sentence of the mother.[152]

This passage shares notable parallels with *Difficulty* 41, such as the interrelatedness of sex and corruption and that corporeal reproduction contravened God's intention. The passage also calls to mind Clement's equation of Eve with pleasure, going so far as to depict her with animalistic language ("she was in heat for pleasure"), further straitening the link between sexual pleasure, the fall, and noetic capitulation to the sensory world. But unlike in Gregory's protology, Maximos gives no indication here that the sexed body had been given to humans in anticipation of the fall. Rather, the connection between pleasure, the sexed body, and the fall is simultaneous.

Difficulty *7.32*

Echoing a few ideas in *Questions and Doubts* 1.3, this *Difficulty* goes further in anticipating major subjects exposited at greater length in *Thalassios* 61 and *Difficulty* 42. The relevant passage in this *Difficulty* is literally a parenthetical aside in a text otherwise hardly concerned with the fall:

> The forefather used his proneness for authority for what is worse, because he diverted his appetite (ὄρεξιν) away from what had been permitted to what had been forbidden (for indeed he was self-determined, but when he had been deceived, he deliberately chose cleaving to the whore (πόρνῃ) and becoming one body (ἓν σῶμα) [with her] instead of cleaving to the Lord and becoming

---

[151] PG 27:240C–D.

[152] *QDoub* 1.3. Compare with the analysis of Bradshaw, "Sexual Difference," 21.

one spirit (ἓν πνεῦμα) [with Him],[153] thus voluntarily alienating himself from the divine and blessed goal, preferring by choice to become dust[154] over being God by grace).[155]

The Confessor describes the fall as the forefather's misdirected appetite toward "what had been forbidden," but never specifies what that was.[156] Presumably, given Maximos' jarring substitution of Eve with a derisive, sex-charged slur, he is referring to intercourse. As in *Questions and Doubts* 1.3, Maximos insinuates that Eve's sensuous provocation was complicit in the transgression, but never spells out how the anthropological partition happened.[157] Puzzlingly, this "forefather" appears as a male singularity that somehow also contains Eve as if she were simultaneously desire itself and his desire for her, which in turn rends his protological unity apart by the wrongful exercise and direction of desire. This sequence is nonetheless consistent with the primal androgyne mythology. Notable also is the dynamic Maximos describes, where Adam must pick between the Unholy Trinity of the female ("the whore"), the corporeal ("one body"), and the material ("dust"), and the Holy Trinity, subtly comprised by the telling terms "Lord" (Son), "spirit" (Holy Spirit), and "God" (the Father). This pattern calls to mind the hierarchical structuring of the cosmos in *Difficulty* 41.2, where female, earthly, and sensible are subordinated to and divided from male, celestial, and intelligible. This androprimal pattern manifestly structures Maximos' exegesis.

The Confessor next relates that this desire ushered in pain, except not as a divine vendetta against the miscreant human[158] but with "the aim that, by undergoing pain we would learn that we have become infatuated (ἐρῶντες) with the non-existent to be taught to redirect this power [of love (ἀγάπη)] to what exists."[159] Here, the Confessor contrasts fleeting infatuation (*eros*) with the sensible world over and against proper love (*agape*) for God. By this logic, though, he co-implicates female impermanence with the ephemerality of eros, and male permanence with eternal *agape*. This pattern yet again reinforces the structure of *Difficulty* 41.2, where the "lesser" (female, inhabited world, earth, and sensible nature) is juxtaposed with the "greater" (male, paradise, heaven, and intelligible nature). In brief, the choice given to the forefather in *Difficulty* 7.32 reflects a similar pattern as the divisions of *Difficulty* 41. From this perspective, it stands to reason to interpret the unification of these divisions, of this anthropological and cosmic fissure, as contingent on female, material, and sensory sublimation into masculine, spiritual, intelligible unity. In other

---

[153] A loose periphrasis of 1 Cor 6:16–17.   [154] Cf. Gen 2:7.   [155] *Diff* 7.32.
[156] Compare with *Diff* 10.60.   [157] Compare with *Thal* 59.12.
[158] See Blowers, *Maximus*, 208–209.   [159] *Diff* 7.32.

words, nothing in this *Difficulty* indicates the permanence of the female – except, perhaps, in sublimated form as the male's rectified pleasure, appetency, and love for the divine. Eve thus functions as a type of dialectical tension in these texts, whose hypostatic permanence is never guaranteed – perhaps never even intended.

Thalassios 61

Maximos takes other approaches to reaching the fundamental human unity protologically shattered by Adam and there, too, we see traces of an impetus to sublimate the female. *Thalassios* 61 is a sustained examination of the fallout from the first human preferring sensory pleasure derived from material creation over intellectual pleasure derived from contemplation of the divine. As Maximos sees it, pain and pleasure are inextricable, so that when the first human sinned and experienced illicit pleasure, he immediately also incurred a debt to pain, since no pain preceded that illicit pleasure to balance the scales, and the pursuit of this pleasure culminates in death (61.2–4).[160] The villain in this text is thus a vicious cycle first caused by pleasure, whereafter the human takes every effort to avoid pain by an indefatigable pursuit of pleasure, which ironically perpetuates the cycle. Christ's incarnation breaks this cycle: By submitting himself to birth in a body liable to pain and death, but without owing a debt to the pleasure that otherwise precedes birth, Christ settles humanity's debt incurred by Adam (61.5–12). While this outline might seemingly marginalize Eve as a concrete person, it hardly absolves her of complicity in this cycle. Rather, her displacement as an individual allows Maximos to conjure her back up in the reconstituted abstraction of pleasure so she can bear the brunt for the Edenic lapse. Eve, in other words, *is* the sensory pleasure that impels the vicious cycle forward that Christ bypasses through his pleasureless birth.

The dilemma begins when the first human, who had been crafted with a "certain potential for noetic pleasure," was drawn to sensory pleasure against his nature "simultaneously with coming into being (ἅμα τῷ γενέσθαι)."[161] Maximos never articulates what this sensory pleasure is, but the fact that its consequences are physical procreation suggests its inextricability from intercourse.[162] Maximos reasons: "After the transgression, all humans naturally had pleasure preceding their own conception (γενέσεως) and there was no one at all who existed free from conception impassioned by pleasure."[163] The exception, naturally, is Christ, who is blameless because "his conception in time from

---

[160] See Larchet, *La divinisation*, 126–131.   [161] *Thal* 61.2.
[162] For further commentary on *Thal* 61, see Larchet, *La divinisation*, 179–181.   [163] *Thal* 61.4.

a woman was in no way constituted by the preceding pleasure from the transgression."[164] So, it does not appear that the hamartiological problem is birth itself – or Christ would be sinful regardless of the mode of conception – but heterosexual reproduction.

Maximos corroborates this point in his tenth *scholion* on *Thalassios* 61: "After the transgression, the origin of human nature was conception from seed after pleasure and birth according to a flow [of blood]."[165] The nod to Aristotelian embryology is evident, but so is the close proximity between pleasure, sex, and procreation as distinguishing marks of the post-Edenic human condition. Nor is this an extraordinary interpretation, considering that, in *Thalassios* 21.2, Maximos had already maintained that after sinning, Adam and humanity in him: "Was condemned to birth propagated through passion and sin, so that thereafter sin originates in the passible part of nature related to birth, as if by a type of law according to which no one is sinless, for all are subject to the law of birth."[166] Here, too, sexual intercourse, sin, and pleasure emerge as inseparable. Conversely, Christ's blamelessness is predicated on the absence of both pleasure and insemination.

However, something is awry in the setup of the central problem. Throughout the text Maximos speaks about sexual pleasure and reproduction without, however, identifying Eve alongside Adam at the moment of the instantaneous fall – in fact, Maximos never uses Eve's name here or in the entirety of *Thalassios*. By all accounts, the narrative begins with a unified and unmistakably male singularity called Adam, but it is entirely unclear how he moves from singularity to multiplicity, or how he reproduces at all – mitosis? – at the exact moment that he comes into existence unless there is always already an internalized and constitutive alterity within him that becomes externalized, indeed, materialized, as a female anthropological excess that must be sublimated afterward to reverse the operation of the instantaneous fall.

We had already seen a similar pattern in Dunning's interpretation of Clement's *Protreptikos* 2, where Dunning shows how Eve acquires a "semi-personified"[167] status in the form of desire. In this way, Clement displaces Eve and refigures her as Adam's own desire that leads him to ruin. In *Thalassios* 61, Maximos appears to follow Clement's lead by displacing Eve with pleasure to uphold an (entirely theoretical) androprimal unity.[168] But at the same time, he resignifies her as Adam's pleasure, which splinters his singularity at the very

---

[164] *Thal* 61.5.   [165] Scholion 10 on Question 61, ll. 51–53.   [166] *Thal* 21.2.
[167] Dunning, *Specters of Paul*, 61.
[168] I limit the examples where Maximos associates the female with pleasure, but other texts make this connection just as explicit, e.g., *QDoub* 125: "By woman, it [a gospel passage] signifies love of pleasure (Διὰ τῆς γυναικὸς ἡ φιληδονία δηλοῦται)."

moment that he begins to exist. Eve, as pleasure, obtains existence in logical simultaneity (ἅμα) with Adam because she signifies the externalization of his pleasure for the sensory world, for her (?), for material reality – that is, with the numerous gendered associations with the female we have already seen Maximos make in other texts, such as *Difficulty* 41. Because this kind of pleasure is concerned with the "lesser," it has a fragmenting, rather than unifying, effect, drawing downward, not upward. Human unity, then, is predicated on the sublimation of pleasure/Eve into the androprimal singularity that logically, but not actually, preceded pleasure/Eve.

So, if we read *Thalassios* 61 from the perspective that Eve has been displaced and resignified as pleasure, the text as a whole rings a different, more troubling, note. For instance, when Maximos contrasts Christ's salvific activity with Adam's ruinous choices, the language is gendered such that blame passes from Adam to a female personification of pleasure. Tellingly, the monastic thinker makes this comparison at 61.7: "For just as Adam's life after pleasure became the mother of death and corruption, so also the death of the Lord on Adam's behalf, which is free from the pleasure of Adam, becomes the sire of eternal life."[169] Here, the turn for the worse introduced by Adam is distinctly cast in female terms, while Christ's redemptive activity is presented as paternal. Maximos puns on Eve's name in the Septuagint when speaking of Adam's Zoe/ life/Eve, who was "after pleasure" (καθ᾽ ἡδονὴν) and who became the "mother of death and corruption." The first instance of life here has a negative sense, a fake sense of vitality and a definitive limitation by death, underscoring the ontological insufficiency of the maternal body. Conversely, Christ's death supersedes the maternal procreative sequence by "siring" eternal life, the "real" kind of life that is free from death since rooted in male vitality. Thus, Maximos contrasts this personified pleasure that, as Eve, has emanated "from Adam" (ἐκ τοῦ Ἀδὰμ) with Christ's death. Maximos does not thereby sideline Eve from the narrative, but obliquely resignifies her as the female force behind sin and fragmentation that must be resolved back into primal male unity through Christ's death. Other passages in *Thalassios* 61 deploy a similar strategy.

For example, at *Thalassios* 61.8, the Confessor continues the association of femininity with pleasure and death, but this time he subtly adds, in addition to procreation, another female-coded task. Maximos bemoans that "procreation from Adam after pleasure was tyrannizing nature, serving food to death through her [i.e., pleasure] (ἡ καθ᾽ ἡδονὴν ἐκ τοῦ Ἀδὰμ γένεσις, τυραννοῦσα τὴν φύσιν, βορὰν τῷ δι᾽ αὐτὴν θανάτῳ παρέπεμπεν)."[170] The dynamics here are again gendered in such a way that culpability becomes displaced onto feminized

---

[169] *Thal* 61.7.   [170] *Thal* 61.8.

personifications. English loses some of this sense, so it bears pointing out that procreation and pleasure are both female, and the former is recast in the feminine participle as "tyrannizing" nature. Maximos additionally warps procreation into a female persona seemingly doubling as a mother and homemaker, who, in a macabre twist of events, is serving death a steady stream of mortal bodies on the platter of the ontological insufficiency that her pleasure and procreative powers literally materialize.

Other passages show a similar adjacency of pleasure and the female as well as the condemnation of human nature to death that results from them. At 61.10, Maximos sighs: "Therefore, death, which was despotically ruling over human nature owing to the transgression, had the pleasure that emanated from the disobedience and that began all procreation according to nature as a pretext for his power, and because of her [i.e., pleasure], death was passed as the sentence of nature."[171] In this short text, the Confessor once more identifies pleasure as the root cause of death, but also of procreation, intimating their coimplication. Similarly so when he continues at 61.11:

> So, because of Adam, who established through his disobedience the law of procreation after pleasure and, because of him, also death as the condemnation of nature, all who have received their being from Adam according to procreation after pleasure necessarily are subject, even if unwilling, to death as a sentence yoked together to nature by virtue of the power of this procreation.[172]

Certainly, Adam is found culpable here – after all, he established the law of procreation through disobedience – but the solution is to deliver *him*, as a synecdoche for humanity, from the clutches of entities entirely personified in female terms, namely, pleasure and procreation.

In sum, *Thalassios* 61 does not so much engage in the unqualified erasure of Eve as much as it resignifies her in the shape of pleasure, which can then be reintegrated and redirected toward the divine. As with *Difficulty* 7.32 and *Questions and Doubts* 1.3, the overarching problematic is Adam's preference of pleasure, the sensory, and the material over the noetic, spiritual, and divine. Because his choice has a fragmenting effect in being directed at the "lesser," unity is achieved by reversing the effects of his decisions through the sublimation of pleasure into the "greater." On its face, this move seems to be a departure from the perhaps more vitriolic statements Maximos sometimes made about Eve and the female sex more generally. But pleasure as a discursively saturated term cannot be so easily extricated from its cultural valences within the Patristic tradition that Maximos is redeploying. Accordingly, it

---

[171] *Thal* 61.10.   [172] *Thal* 61.11.

would be disingenuous to interpret the Confessor's proposed resolution to Adam's "pleasure" as somehow entirely separate from the signifying economy that implicated pleasure with the female, and, in this text especially, with the contingency of human life on female reproductive power.

Mary

Like most Christian Romans, Maximos held Mary in the highest regard possible for his culture, but her status as the Theotokos, or God-bearer, did little to elevate her past his beliefs about her sex. Even though Maximos aims to bypass the standard Aristotelian reproductive economy (i.e., male/seed/activity, female/blood/passivity) in the soteriological drama, he still regards Mary as the paradoxically virginal purveyor of Christ's flesh and Christ as seed of himself. This proposition is logically fraught, and we can only assume that Maximos espouses it because he failed to conceive of alternatives beyond Aristotelian embryological grammar. Maximos further views Christ's body, because birthed by a woman, as ontologically insufficient and eschatologically wanting: Only the body resurrected by the Father is ultimately perfect. So, in this exegetical dilemma, Mary remains hermeneutically inflected and constrained by the androprimacy at the heart of Hellenic medical anthropology. In fairness, the Confessor expressed the great mystery of the incarnation with the scientific language available to him, and within these parameters, he produced a mostly coherent account. But the discursive insufficiencies of the language itself made it impossible to produce as ambitious an account of human sexlessness as he set out to articulate in *Difficulty* 41 and elsewhere. Thus, his anthropogenic model and eschatological vision remain destabilized by the logic of androprimacy, which reasserts itself through Christ's vital agency in directing his own gestation in Mary. In the end, these supernatural reproductive schematics remain a paraphrased Aristotelian androprimal embryology.

Difficulty *42*

This *Difficulty* is concerned with resolving the problem of bodily reproduction as Maximos understands it. As *Thalassios* 61, *Difficulty* 42 intimates that corporeal reproduction happened at the exact moment of creation owing to desire for the sensory (*Diff* 42.7). But in this text, the Confessor focuses less on juridical debt and more on the dialectic of ethics and ontology vis-à-vis reproduction. The text is fairly complex, so I offer a brief outline before discussing the relevant sections. The central conundrum of *Difficulty* 42 is that Adam's transgression subjected all of humanity to nonrational, nonspiritual material reproduction, meaning reproduction by seed as plants and blood as animals

(42.7). This kind of reproduction is ethically compromised because it hinges on directing one's desire toward "wickedness" and away from God (42.7). Because this unnatural movement occurred simultaneously with the creation of humanity, humanity never existed without this condition (42.7). As a consequence of this form of reproduction, humans subsequently born from other bodies become inescapably liable to sins, passions, and death. However, because Christ does not assume human flesh from seed as other humans (42.11), his flesh is only liable to the consequences of sin (i.e., the blameless passions of the fallen body) but not to sin itself (42.3). Maximos' objective here is to show that Christ preserves a perfect typological parallel with Adam insofar as he has the sinlessness of the first human but also the postlapsarian flesh subject to the passions that followed from the transgression (42.3–4). Thus, Christ heals human nature from within its fallen state by liberating it from corporeal reproduction, which is involuntary and impassioned, and in its stead offers a free and chaste spiritual birth through the grace of baptism and adoption in the Spirit. This last form of birth from the Spirit is the original nonmaterial, spiritual, and divine form of reproduction God had intended for humanity with the goal of deification (42.25, 31).

Two key terms here, "seed" and "blood," effectively function as an Aristotelian synecdoche for the male and female reproductive functions by which humanity has abased itself in becoming unnaturally and irrationally continuous with the vegetative and animal spectrum of life. While Maximos indicates several times that sin is somehow associated with corporeal reproduction and, to that degree, with some form of lust (42.3–7, 25, 31), his main point here is that Christ's unique birth makes it possible to sublimate the corporeal birth into a spiritual, nonmaterial form of reproduction. This sequence, in turn, mirrors a similar progression as that previously examined in *Difficulty* 41. In that text, the expectation was also an upward sequence whereby the "lesser" (the female, material, sensory, corporeal) are resolved into the "higher" (spiritual, immaterial, divine, etc.). As we see in brief, however, Maximos jettisons the transcendence of *all* sexual difference and jibes downwind into the conceptually hospitable haven of androprimacy.

The first of several sustained typologies between Adam and Christ appears early on in the *Difficulty* as Maximos attempts to explain two phrases in Gregory of Nazianzos' *Oration on Baptism* that are too complex and tangential to dwell on here. For our purposes, what matters is that Maximos regards the form of corporeal reproduction introduced by Adam as leading to sin and corruption. Christ's incarnation and resurrection remedy the human plight by making birth from baptism and resurrection possible in lieu of birth from matter and bodies:

> By accepting creaturely origin on the one hand, He was naturally identified with the human through the *life-giving inbreathing* (Wis 15:11), through which, in assuming the uncompromised and spotless *image* (Gen 1:26), He remained as a human possessing the freedom of sinlessness. On the other hand, by accepting birth in the flesh, that is, by willingly clothing Himself in the *form of the slave* (Phlp 2:7), so as to assume the *likeness* of the corrupted *human* (Heb 2:14), the Sinless One, as though liable for sin, subjected Himself to natural passions *akin to* ours by His will, but *without sin* (Heb 4:15). For He was compounded in accordance with these aspects and from out of these aspects of ours, and became perfectly a new *Adam*, bearing in Himself *the first Adam* (1 Cor 15:45) undiminished in both aspects.[173]

Here Maximos shows Christ's simultaneous continuity with and difference from Adam by satisfying two criteria: innocence from sin through God's inbreathing as the first Adam before the transgression and the assumption of the body that Adam had after the transgression, distinguished by its liability to corruption, death, and the natural passions. This second criterion shows that birth from a (presumably female) body, even if morally sinless, still results in a postlapsarian body liable to the passions. Therefore, bodies born from bodies, even if sinless, must still be elevated by the Father into their eschatological condition. If so, this position forecloses any corporeal interpretation of "be fruitful and multiply" (Gen 1:28), as corporeal reproduction categorically entails lust for procreation and eschatological transfiguration.[174] Even Christ's body must receive incorruptibility, freedom from the natural passions, and immortality *after* the resurrection, after, that is, the Father's intervention to elevate the lowly status ("enslaved," "corrupted") of Christ's body materialized by Mary. The outcome is twofold: First, Christ's moral perfection as a human is guaranteed by the Father's inbreathing of the Spirit; second, Christ's corporeal perfection as a human is conditional on the resurrection, not on the Theotokos' virginal and sinless body. If so, here too a similar pattern as in *Difficulty* 41 emerges, whereby the woman's ontological insufficiency is tacitly affirmed, even if that woman is the Theotokos.

A similar pattern recurs in the same *Difficulty*, where Maximos uses a strategy of resignifying Eve akin to that in *Thalassios* 61 that codes nature as a female

---

[173] *Diff* 42.3.

[174] Maximos seems inconsistent regarding the sexual act, as in some texts (e.g., *QDoub* 183, *ChL* 2.17) he regards it grudgingly as potentially good if directed at reproduction, whereas in this text and in *Thal* 61, sex, sin, and the fallen body seem inextricable.

quasi-subject needing transcendence into a higher state. To draw this meaning out, I follow the underlying Greek in rendering "nature" as female.

> So it was from being condemned to reproduction through seed like grass and from obtaining our life through blood like the rest of the animals, that the Lord, Who heals human nature and returns her to her primordial grace of incorruptibility, came to liberate her – to manifest clearly to her the beauty toward which she utterly failed to move at the very beginnings when she came into being, and to trample down the wickedness toward which she unnaturally moved through the deception simultaneously with her being created.[175]

The salvific agent is here once more cast in distinctly masculine terms as the Lord, who elevates the "lesser" subject, the female-coded nature, into a higher state ("the primordial grace of incorruptibility") that ostensibly lies beyond sexual difference (male/seed, female/blood). The Confessor achieves this symbolic effect by subtly juxtaposing the male-coded Lord over and against the female-coded nature. This juxtaposition associates the Lord with the promise made to Eve that her offspring (the Lord) will "trample" (πατῆσαι) the serpent's head (i.e., "wickedness"), while conversely associating fallen nature with Eve "through the deception" (διὰ τῆς ἀπάτης) that is intertextually linked with her (Gen 3:1–6, 1 Tim 2:12–14). Christ's salvific mission culminates by "binding the power of human desire to himself," thus achieving a similar outcome as in *Difficulty* 41: the transcendence of sexual differentiation (male/seed, female/blood) by attaining the androprimally-coded apex of ontological ascent through desire for the male ("the Lord").

To achieve this outcome, Maximos proposes a mode of reproduction that bypasses bodies with greater detail than his insinuation to the same effect in *Difficulty* 41.7. For example, in 42.25, he elucidates what it means for Christ to introduce a new aspect to human existence: "So that the only new aspect he introduced was the innovation of nature, by which I mean his conception without seed and his birth without corruption, from which features nature was separated after the fall, having plummeted away from the divine and spiritual mode of reproduction into a multiplicity."[176] On first glance, this passage seems to replicate the logic that would eliminate both the female and male elements from the human in the hopes of attaining a higher, ostensibly sexless, state, that of the "divine and spiritual mode of reproduction." But this solution only works if we assume that matter, the sensory, is not culturally associated with the female any more than the spiritual and divine is with the male. That is hardly the case, of course, as the Confessor later shows in 42.31, where he uses language

---

[175] *Diff* 42.7.   [176] *Diff* 42.25.

strongly reminiscent of the five divisions of *Difficulty* 41 and the hierarchization of their contents:

> When the first human overlooked this deifying, divine, and immaterial birth in preferring what was pleasant and superficial instead of intellectual blessings that were not yet evident, he was condemned to have an involuntary, material, and mortal birth from bodies, since God justly determined that he who freely chose the lesser over the greater (τῶν κρειττόνων τὰ χείρονα) should exchange his free, dispassionate, self-determined, and pure birth for an impassioned, enslaved, and compelled birth *after the likeness of the irrational and mindless animals* (Ps 49:13 LXX) of the earth.[177]

If the "deifying, divine, and immaterial birth" is meant to be a means of overcoming sexual differentiation, it is telling that it is primarily differentiated from what Maximos had earlier associated with the female, and the lower element of each hierarchy, in *Difficulty* 41.2. In fact, the Confessor uses the exact same phrase in referring to the first human's preference of "the lesser over the greater (τῶν κρειττόνων τὰ χείρονα)." This text thus deploys the same logic of *Difficulty* 41, where the relative abstractness of "male and female" discussed there becomes here a more concrete problematic anchored in the embarrassment of animalistic corporeal birth.

The theoretical discussion of eradicating corporeal birth is far from innocent, especially given that, if successful, it eliminates any female raison d'être within Maximos' cultural parameters. This observation is no exaggeration, considering the appallingly sustained history of Greco-Romans who regularly and unironically pondered the ontological superfluity of women. For example, in the following passage Theodoretos of Kyrrhos approvingly echoes Gregory of Nyssa's suggestion that God made sexed bodies in anticipation of the fall but adds an insulting but telltale coda:

> Having foreseen and foreknown Adam's affairs – how he would become mortal after having transgressed the commandment – he prepared his nature beforehand such that he structured the shape of the body into male and female; the fashioning of the mortal bodies was such owing to the need for child-making for the preservation of the species, for immortal nature has no need of the female.[178]

This is not the sole time that Theodoretos casually floated women's disposability, nor were such ethical obscenities uncommon.[179] So, even if Maximos does

---

[177] *Diff* 42.31, emphasis mine.
[178] Theodoretos of Kyrros, *Questions on the Octateuch,* 37–38: 8–15, Marcos and Sáenz-Badillos, eds.
[179] E.g., *Compendium of Heretical Fables*, PG 83:472A.

not expressly articulate this precise position, is it really that radical to suggest that he somehow eschatologically anticipates it?

After all, the core of Maximos' exposition of the Adam–Christ typology is bookended by a unified male singularity on either end that once again stands on male primacy, even autogenesis.[180] This mythology appears with particular clarity in Christ's conception. At issue is Christ's preservation of continuity between the old and new Adam, while circumventing sinful means of procreation:

> For just as the teacher [Gregory Nazianzen] himself says, "after God took the body from matter, which had obviously just been made, and after imbuing it with life from Himself (which indeed, according to scripture, is the rational *soul* and *image of God*, [Gen 1:26]), He fashions a human," in the same way "after taking a body" from an unblemished virgin, as if from undefiled earth, "and having imbued it with life from Himself (which indeed, according to scripture, is the rational *soul* and *image of God*, [Gen 1:26]), He created His own humanity," or, having willingly and for our sake – as He is omnipotent – assumed intellectually- and rationally-ensouled flesh, He changelessly made Himself be fashioned into a human.[181]

The imagery that compares Mary's body to the pristine soil from which the first Adam was fashioned had a long history in Patristic elucidations of the Adam–Christ typology, going back at the very least to Irenaios of Lyon.[182] Maximos is firmly situated in this tradition, as he now refigures Mary by materializing her into the soil from which Christ's body is constituted.

In this, Maximos seems tacitly committed not to acknowledge maternal or female priority over the male. Most likely, Maximos is pressed into this corner because female priority is irreconcilable with the underlying mythology of androprimacy. So, while Adam and Christ are both preceded by a female figure, either as the soil of the newly created world, from which Adam is made, or as the virginal body of Mary, from whom Christ is born, Maximos will nonetheless find ways of subverting their precedence over the males. In the case of Adam, the soil itself is preceded by God and is passively handled by God to make the first human, thereby replicating gendered stereotypes of the maternal body as material and passive and of the male as active and giving form. By the same logic, Mary's body precedes Christ's insofar as his is taken from hers, but she is regardless treated passively, as a material substrate, who is literally compared to inert soil. Rather, God fashions himself in the Theotokos' body, as the seed,

---

[180] Judith Butler uses the term "male autogenesis" in *Bodies That Matter*, 54, while examining Plato's *Timaios*. I believe a similar structure is at work in Christian texts from late antiquity, not only in relation to Adam and Christ but ultimately going back to the ungeneratedness of the Godhead.

[181] *Diff* 42.11.

[182] See Dunning, *Specters of Paul*, 97–123; Behr, *Asceticism and Anthropology*, 58–74.

once again to preserve the logic of androprimacy even if it means having to fall back on the very Aristotelian embryology and reproductive logic that Maximos is attempting to avoid here.

Precisely at this point the Confessor runs into an impasse out of his commitment to maintain the myth of androprimacy while also trying to find a workaround solution to the ancestral condemnation and its consequences. Let's review: The objective of *Difficulty* 42 was to overcome postlapsarian birth conditioned by seed and blood, which Christ ostensibly does by being conceived without seed. But even if we grant that being born of Mary without seed somehow solves the problem of impassioned reproduction, it does not overcome the embryological principles of insemination, since Christ functions as the seed he is meant to displace and still concocts himself from the holy Virgin's blood. For this reason, Maximos expressly claims that Christ "created His own humanity" and "made Himself be fashioned into a human" in Mary's womb. But, by returning to Aristotle's reproductive biomechanics, this *Difficulty* fails to elude its commitments to the totalizing masculinity of Greco-Roman Christian androprimacy. This is also apparent in the implication that Christ still fashions himself out of the virginal blood, and that his body is corruptible, even in the absence of the pleasure that precedes insemination. Therefore, even if we concede that Maximos is attempting to transcend female *and male*, his solution gravitates once more to the ineluctably axiomatic pull of Aristotelian embryological androprimacy, which in turn compromises his narrative's coherence by presupposing premises categorically irreconcilable with any articulation of human sexlessness. In the end, the male principle is simply transposed onto Christ, which in turn underlines Mary's inability to direct the gestation of Christ's body or, indeed, to give him a body that is not already ontologically marred by the inferior constitution of all bodies born of women.

Questions and Doubts 33

The association between Christ and the male gestating principle is even clearer in other texts. For example, *Questions and Doubts* 33 explains the symbology of Jephthah and his daughter (Jdgs 11:34–38) as representing Christ and his flesh. The passage once more falls into the gendered pattern that feminizes the flesh and body, while masculinizing Christ. But this text goes further, claiming that Christ "sinlessly came forth according to the flesh from our prostituted nature and became the Begetter of His very own flesh."[183] Associating nature with sexual malfeasance resonates with other texts already

---

[183] *QDoub* 33.

examined, such as *Difficulty* 7.32, where Maximos calls Eve a sexually charged expletive, or *Difficulty* 42.7, where Maximos feminizes nature while tying it closely, through calculated word choice, with Eve. But what matters most here is the Confessor's reference to Christ as "having become the begetter of His very own flesh" (τῆς οἰκείας σαρκὸς γενόμενος σπορεύς). The association is closer in Greek, where the "begetter" (σπορεύς) could equally be called the "sower" or, more woodenly and awkwardly, the "inseminator." This text is brief and does not dwell at length on what it means that Christ begets his own flesh. But that hardly matters as the text unambiguously affirms Christ as the male, animating, form-giving principle of his own gestation in keeping with Aristotelian embryology. Thus, we find a similar structure here as in *Difficulty* 41, where even if there is a certain bypassing of the female (blood) and the male (seed) principles, they are still resolved into a higher, divine, unified state that itself fails to avoid the reinscription of masculinity where it must be absent for logical consistency.

Difficulty 5

While exegeting Dionysios' *Letter* 4, Maximos affirms that to "innovate the laws of natural birth," Christ has to become human without the "seed of the male," so that Mary "'in a manner beyond nature, conceived' the 'Word Who is beyond being, shaped into human form from her virginal blood without the participation of a man,' by a strange ordinance contrary to nature."[184] Here Christ is formed from the Virgin's blood, in conventional Aristotelian fashion, albeit without seed, which Maximos perceptively describes as a "strange ordinance contrary to nature." Nonetheless, the Confessor will again fall back on Aristotelian embryological biomechanics to underscore Christ's self-formation in Mary by identifying him with his own seed, as in *Difficulty* 42 and *Questions and Doubts* 33.

This last point becomes especially apparent at 5.13, where Maximos elucidates the dynamics of Christ's incarnation:

> *While being beyond substance*, therefore, *He was substantialized* when He fashioned in nature a different beginning of origination and birth[185] inasmuch as He was conceived when He became the seed of His own flesh (σπορὰ τῆς οἰκείας σαρκὸς), while being born when He became the seal of the virginity of the bearer, showing in her case the contradiction of mutually-exclusive terms that are simultaneously true. For the same one is both virgin and mother, innovating nature by the coincidence of opposites – given that virginity and birth pertain to opposites, the convergence of which no one

---

[184] *Diff* 5.6.   [185] See Wis 7:5.

could have contrived on the basis of nature. Therefore, the Virgin is truly also Theotokos (since she supernaturally conceived, as though by seed (δίκην σπορᾶς), and bore the supersubstantial Word), precisely because the one who bears is properly mother of the one sown (σπαρέντος) and conceived.[186]

This text recalls various themes discussed in earlier texts, such as the concern with circumventing conception without male seed, or the emphasis on virginity, or birth without corruption, all in the interest of innovating postlapsarian human nature. But what is particularly telling of the central importance of androprimacy in this salvific schema is the Confessor's repeated identification of Christ as the animating cause of himself in the Theotokos' womb. Maximos seems aware that this association is fraught given the importance he had earlier attributed to Christ's seedless reproduction (5.6), as in earlier texts (e.g., *Thalassios* 61, *Difficulty* 42). So, he attempts to soften his statement with "as though by seed" to indicate a metaphorical register that nonetheless fails to circumvent the logical faux pas.

In summary, then, Maximos missed a constructive opportunity that he himself set out to postulate, and one that perhaps already insinuated itself within his expansive theological anthropology. His argument required him to bypass the biological reproductive sequence that characterizes the fallen cosmos by holding up instead the paradoxical events that took place in Christ's conception. But rather than leaning into the paradoxically nonsexually fecund possibilities germinating in the mode of Christ's unique conception, Maximos resorted to the conceptually limiting and androprimacy-driven embryology of Aristotle, thereby foreclosing further speculation into the very alternatives to embodied existence that he so tantalizingly entertained but did not deliver on in *Difficulty* 41.7. If that is true, does the Confessor's failure in this specific aspect burden his interpreters to deliver on his unfulfilled promise by using their hindsight to elude, though certainly not their own, at least his epistemological strictures?

Conclusion

The Adam–Christ typology that persists in the background of the texts examined in this section can only work by the somewhat forceful imposition of the discourse of androprimacy. Androprimacy, due to its inextricable association with masculinist assumptions, fails to signify beyond itself and thereby does not deliver on the promise of sexlessness the Confessor aspires to in *Difficulty* 41 and elsewhere. While it is true that the male singularity prevails in the form of Christ, especially as refigured as the seed, the actively animating male principle of his own gestation, even this singularity does not entirely extricate itself from

---

[186] *Diff* 5.13.

gendered multivalences. Rather, female erasure remains inchoate in this articulation because desire and materiality, as functional refigurations of Eve and Mary, remain ineradicable in the Christic singularity that sublimates them. Humanity's desire for the divine endures as a perpetual force in the ever-moving repose around God,[187] just as much as Christ eternally remains the fruit of Mary's womb.

From this perspective, Maximos fails to produce an entirely satisfactory narrative for the structure he proposes, moving from (male) singularity to (sexually differentiated) multiplicity and back to (male) singularity. The monad Maximos proposes only relegates sexual difference to another semantic register and thereby never resolves it in its new refigurations. What can be said with certainty, though, is that however semantically inflected, the Confessor's eschatology remains committed to androprimacy, here finally emerging as a form of supremacy and totalizing finality predicated on its implied ontological priority. So, even if the vestigial feminine remains, it remains forever sublimated, subsumed, and subdued within and under the male, possessing no more than an uncertain identity of its own. If so, it is difficult to imagine how such a conclusion, one that stretches the sex-based inequities of the fallen cosmos to the eons of infinity, could function without critical recalibration as the ground for a constructive project with feminist and/or queer sensitivities.

Conclusion

In *Difficulty* 67, Maximos explains the difference between "means" and "extremes" while discussing the numerology behind the loaves of bread with which Christ fed the multitudes. At 67.10, he offers a peculiar example to illustrate the difference: "An 'extreme' is: *And God said, Let us make the human according to Our image and likeness.* A 'mean' is: *And God made the human, male and female He made them.* And once more, an 'extreme' is: *In Christ Jesus there is neither male nor female.*"[188] I find this example illuminating for the central argument of this Element, as it neatly encapsulates Maximos' most basic understanding of sexual difference as an ephemeral (and unnecessary) stage enfolded on the one end by the originally unified human that was rent asunder into sexual difference at the fall and on the other end the unified humanity anticipated in Christ's resurrected body. Here, the male monad that moves to the sexually differentiated dyad is once again resolved into the male monad. In this explanation, Maximos leans on Philo's *On the Creation of the World*, where the Alexandrian explains that male is signified by odd and female by even numbers.[189] It is likely that Maximos understands the dyad similarly,

---

[187] *Thal* 59.8.   [188] *Diff* 67.10.   [189] Philo, *On the Creation of the World*, 3.13.

namely, as a female excess sublimated into a male singularity, which shows yet again the prevailing force of androprimacy in structuring religious exegesis.

By contrast with my central thesis in this volume, there have been numerous interpretations of Maximos' striking claims about the ephemerality and unnaturalness of sexual difference, including a synthesis of the sexes, the pacification of their adversarial agonism, psychological metaphorization, constructive alternatives, and the constatation that Maximos truly envisions the eradication of sexual difference. The introduction aimed to identify the merits and explanatory gaps in these various positions and to propose an alternative. While my argument concurs with the last interpretation, I have maintained that the story does not end there. Rather, it ends in a totalizing male eschaton where sexual difference is purportedly eradicated by resolving all difference into male monism. I then offered an overview of Maximos' medical-anthropological and exegetical context to show that the concurrence of these two traditions, particularly as mediated through Pauline androcentric typology, resulted in the Confessor's largely subtle, but still identifiable, vision of an eschaton the alleged sexlessness of which is subverted by the reinscription of masculinity.

I showed, through a close reading of key Maximian texts, how the Confessor's logical structure of androprimacy determines the aforementioned outcome, both in the eschatology he posits in *Difficulty* 41, where the "lesser" female is sublimated into the "greater" male (along with some of the other divisions that are correspondingly gendered), and in his exegesis of Eve and Mary, who likewise become hypostatically translucent in favor of their more ontologically opaque male counterparts, Adam and Christ. However, the outcome was not quite as logically consistent as Maximos had perhaps wished. For one, there remains the fact that his eschatology fails to be satisfactorily sexless given the male-coded remainder. Indeed, the eschatological male itself remains identifiable as such precisely because the female in its refigurations and resignifications refuses to be entirely effaced. In other words, the male is only intelligible because its constitutive alterities endure in some guise. This much was especially evident in the Confessor's exegesis of Eve, who survives eschatological erasure in the shape of desire, just as much as Mary's materiality persists in Christ's.

These findings lead me to a similar conclusion as that reached by Benjamin Dunning's study of sexual difference in a variety of early Christian texts that partly defined Maximos' own position, as we have seen.[190] Dunning concludes that the variously failed early Christian attempts to produce a fully coherent account of the meaning and end of sexual difference signal "not a total and

---

[190] I must also underline how much Dunning's thinking, as my former professor and as a scholar, has aided my own work in this Element.

inassimilable alterity . . . but rather a necessary instability in the very categories that constitute theological anthropology."[191] If so, Dunning continues, "the failure to produce a *definitive* story for sexually differentiated theological anthropology has the potential to force open the space for other kinds of stories."[192] That is, the impossibility of epistemological closure that attends the never-ending negotiation of the status and significance of the sexually differentiated body can thus become a creative force for unexplored possibilities. Some of these already insinuate themselves from within Maximos' own most adventurous speculations.

First, as I promised in the introduction, the consequences of examining Maximos' understanding of sexual difference have broader consequences than solely the human register. Because of humanity's mediatory and microcosmic role, all that is true of humanity has universal implications. The Confessor is well-known for his comparatively positive view of the world and its divine destiny. But a caution is in order here: The structure of androprimacy that governs Maximos' discussions of sexual difference shares parallels across the cosmic order, as we saw in the gendering of the five divisions in *Difficulty* 41. Accordingly, it bears inquiring whether some of the troubling dimensions of female sublimation and attempted erasure that we underlined in the fifth division are replicated across the other four. An ecofeminist project naturally suggests itself here, but it is one that should be shored up with native resources, such as Maximos' development of the "union without confusion" of the Fourth Ecumenical Council. This much is necessary if, as is clear from Maximos' writings, a unique *logos* exists, not only of every human person but of every organism, from the frailty of newborn fauna to the irreplicable fractal beauty of the vegetative realm. These, too, endure in some way in their individuated uniqueness by the power of Christ's union without confusion with the totality of created nature. In turn, we must reflect carefully on how our various expositions of Maximos' thought perhaps unawares replicate or further the revenant specter of androprimacy in the anthropological continuum and beyond, perhaps especially by legitimating the subjection, rather than the dignified treatment, of a natural world that is also part of divine self-disclosure.

Second, it would be difficult to overstate the constructive possibilities Maximos made available by denaturalizing sexual categories. I am unaware of any earlier Christian denying the natural status of sex more clearly or within a more rigorous philosophical framework, and it is perhaps this mere fact that has called so much scholarly attention to Maximos. Although I have noted that in the end the Confessor remains strapped by the strictures of androprimacy as

---

[191] Dunning, *Specters of Paul*, 154.   [192] Dunning, *Specters of Paul*, 155.

he attempts to posit sexlessness, it bears pondering whether his devoted interpreters do not bear a responsibility to the Confessor analogous to that which Maximos assumed with regard to Gregory and Dionysios in the *Difficulties*. In other words, is there a way in which Maximos' attempt to conceptualize human sexlessness beyond female *and male* should be expressed anew, perhaps unburdened by the categories of Greek medicine and androcentric exegesis?

Perhaps we might begin by recognizing that Maximos' distinction between *logos* and *tropos* is in fact quite useful for framing the issue of sexual difference in contemporary discourse. Because there is no *logos* of male or female (or any other gender category), no person is ontologically or ethically bound to conform to an idea eternally pre-contained in the divine mind that dictates – with eternal consequences – the essential parameters of their sexual or gender identity. This point bears restating. For Maximos, there is no essential and divinely ordained quality in any human being that obliges quotidian adherence to a specific sexed or gendered category. "Male" and "female," just as any sexual category in any time, place, culture, or language, are arbitrary constructions of human phenomena defined by a certain epistemological optic. This point alone should be sufficient grounds for positing a range of constructive feminist and queer projects; I can merely hint at a few here.

The popular claims in certain apostolic traditions that women must be excluded from the clergy on account of their sex presuppose an essentialism and referential stability that can be questioned on the basis of unexplored possibilities embedded within these same apostolic traditions. The price for becoming clergy should never be the reduction of an identity to a restrictive class (such as "male" or "masculinity"), but rather an expansion of the ontological register of the "human." That is what the Confessor advocated for, even if his better efforts were incapacitated by his cultural limitations. Conversely, Maximos, as a monastic, was at best apprehensive of heterosexual unions and was clearly torn about the moral status of the sexual act. He himself evidently preferred a same-sex monastic union with Anastasios, which lasted more than five decades. Doubtless, in the long-term unavoidable and multi-dimensional intimacy of such a partnership, the Confessor learned the virtue-building value of proximity with another person regardless of the fact that they were both male. In other words, it is as harmful as it is misguided to believe that committed and intimate relationships of one combination of sexual identities are categorically productive of deifying virtues, whereas others, of a different combination of sexual identities, are categorically incapable of doing so. A relationship's divinizing potential within the indigenous Christian traditions that attend to the teachings of Maximos should not be measured by obsequious reproductive compatibility but by the power for love, justice, kindness, and the other virtues that they reciprocally foster in the individuals that consensually form it.

There remains one final point I promised to take up again, and that is the sexual identity of Christ. Here again we are faced with the intractable contradiction of Maximos' more adventurous speculation and the epistemologically restrictive features of his culture's androprimacy. On the one hand, it would be truly difficult to pretend that Christ is not male throughout Maximos' corpus and in the bulk of the Christian tradition. In every meaningful regard, Maximos handles Christ as a male individual. And yet, what if Maximos also meant, as he appears to, that Christ did not need to be female or male to be incarnate – and indeed, that Christ in the incarnation was in fact neither? This possibility deserves its own lengthy exploration, which I leave for a different volume. For now, it should be enough to offer some closing thoughts based on this intriguing possibility.

If Christ cannot be regarded as male – or not only as male – then the argument for all-male clergy in some traditions that is predicated on the exclusive sexual continuity between Christ and the male ecclesiastical hierarchies becomes meritless, as are other, more minor, customs that equally trace their justifications to the same rationale. Further, the incarnation is potentially the queerest moment in Christian history as the moment of divine intervention that shatters the reification of ontologically limiting categories. The Confessor had already called attention to the numerous ways in which the thresholds of nature caved in on themselves in the incarnation. But what if we take the claim seriously that the incarnation is the moment that overturns the arbitrary materialization of sexual difference, itself ostensibly a result of the fall? God's hypostatic union with humanity subjects humanity, by the reciprocity of predicates, to the same apophatic deferral of epistemological closure that characterizes the divine itself. Perhaps that elusive quality of the divine, its incircumscribability, becomes in the incarnation the fulfillment of the deferred atavistic promise to fashion humanity in the divine image, that is, to finally deliver humanity from the reductive definitions that compromise the meaning, content, and beauty of being a person.

Abbreviations of Maximos the Confessor's Works

Comm:	*Commentary on the Lord's Prayer*
Diff:	*Difficulties* (aka *The Ambigua*)
Ep:	*Epistles*
ChL:	*Four Hundred Chapters on Love*
QDoub:	*Questions and Doubts*
Thal:	*Questions and Answers to Thalassios*
ChTh:	*Two Hundred Chapters on Theology*

A few notes:

Laga and Steel's critical editions of *Questions and Answer to Thalassios* have no paragraph subdivisions, so I use the subdivisions of Maximos (Nicholas) Constas' English translation.

Maximos' *Epistles* have no critical edition, so I use the *PG* text.

Otherwise, I use the most updated editions of Maximos' and all other ancient texts as found on the *Thesaurus Linguae Graecae*, and follow their standard sectional divisions.

I use English, sometimes Greek, but not Latin, to refer to Greek titles.

I use "Roman" to refer to the peoples of the Roman Empire, including the eastern Romans whom others might recognize by their colonially inflected pejorative: "Byzantine."

All translations are mine, even though incomparably better versions abound. The reason is to offer consistency of translation style to this Element, as well as sometimes to highlight peculiarities about a text. Thus, the reader can also be assured that any lack of clarity, obtuseness, or error in the English rendition of other languages rests squarely on my shoulders.

Bibliography

Aimilianos of Simonopetra. *The Mystical Marriage: Spiritual Life according to St. Maximos the Confessor*. Columbia, NY: Newrome Press, 2018.

Andreou, Andria. "'Emotioning' Gender," in *Emotions and Gender in Byzantine Culture*, Stavroula Constantinou and Mati Meyer, eds. Cham: Palgrave MacMillan, 2019, 35–63.

Balthasar, Hans Urs von. *Kosmische Liturgie: Das Weltbild Maximus' des Bekenners*. Einsiedeln: Johannes-Verlag, 1988.

Behr, John. *Asceticism and Anthropology in Irenaeus and Clement*. Oxford: Oxford University Press, 2000.

Berthold, George. "Did Maximus the Confessor Know Augustine?" *Studia Patristica* 17.1 (1982): 14–17.

Betancourt, Roland. *Byzantine Intersectionality: Sexuality, Gender, and Race in the Middle Ages*. Princeton: Princeton University Press, 2020.

Blowers, Paul. "Gentiles of the Soul: Maximus the Confessor on the Substructure and Transformation of Human Passions," *Journal of Early Christian Studies* 4.1 (1996): 57–85.

"The Dialectics and Therapeutics of Desire in Maximus the Confessor," *Vigiliae Christianae* 65 (2011): 425–451.

Maximus the Confessor: Jesus Christ and the Transfiguration of the World. Oxford: Oxford University Press, 2016.

Booth, Phil. *Crisis of Empire: Doctrine and Dissent at the End of Late Antiquity*. Berkeley, CA: University of California Press, 2014.

Boyarin, Daniel. *A Radical Jew: Paul and the Politics of Identity*. Berkeley, CA: University of California Press, 1994.

Bradshaw, David. "Sexual Difference and the Difference It Makes," in *The Reception of Greek Ethics in Late Antiquity and Byzantium*. Sophia Xenophontos and Anna Marmodoro, eds. Cambridge: Cambridge University Press, 2021, 15–35.

Brock, Sebastian and Susan Harvey, trans. *Holy Women of the Syrian Orient*. Berkeley, CA: University of California Press, 1987.

Brown, Peter. *The Body and Society: Men, Women, and Sexual Renunciation in Early Christianity*. New York: Columbia University Press, 1988.

Butler, Judith. *Gender Trouble: Feminism and the Subversion of Identity*. London: Routledge, 1990.

Bodies that Matter: On the Discursive Limits of Sex. London: Routledge, 1993.

Cadden, Joan. *Meanings of Sex Difference in the Middle Ages: Medicine, Science, and Culture* Cambridge: Cambridge University Press, 1993.

Cobb, Stephanie. *Dying to Be Men: Gender and Language in Early Christian Martyr Texts*. New York: Columbia University Press, 2008.

Cohn, Leopold., ed. *Philonis Alexandrini opera quae supersunt* 1. Berlin: Reimer, 1896.

Connell, Sophia. *Aristotle on Women: Physiology, Psychology, and Politics*. Cambridge: Cambridge University Press, 2021.

Constas, Nicholas, trans. *On Difficulties in Sacred Scripture: The Responses to Thalassios*. Washington, DC: Catholic University of America Press, 2018.

ed. and trans. *On Difficulties in the Church Fathers: The Ambigua*, vols. 1 and 2. Cambridge, MA: Harvard University Press, 2014.

Conway, Colleen. *Behold the Man: Jesus and Greco-Roman Masculinity*. Oxford: Oxford University Press, 2008.

Cooper, Adam. *Holy Flesh, Wholly Deified: The Body in St Maximus the Confessor*. Oxford: Oxford University Press, 2005.

Costache, Doru. "Living above Gender: Insights from Saint Maximus the Confessor," *Journal of Early Christian Studies* 21.2 (2013): 261–290.

Cvetković, Vladimir. "Logoi, Porphyrian Tree, and Maximus the Confessor's Rethinking of Aristotelian Logic," in *Aristotle in Byzantium*, Mikonja Knežević, ed. Alhambra, CA: Sebastian Press, 2020, 191–215.

"Sex, Gender, and Christian Identity in the Patristic Era," *Philosophy and Society* 32.2 (2021): 162–176.

Davis, Stephen. "Crossed Texts, Crossed Sex: Intertextuality in Early Christian Legends of Holy Women Disguised as Men," *Journal of Early Christian Studies* 10.1 (2002): 1–36.

Derrida, Jacques. "La pharmacie de Platon," *Tel Quel* 32–33, (1968): 256–367.

Derrida, Jacques. *Dissemination*. Barbara Johnson, ed. and trans. Chicago, IL: University of Chicago Press, 1981, 61–171.

Dewhurst, Brown E. "The Absence of Sexual Difference in the Theology of Maximus the Confessor," *Philosophy and Society* 32.2 (2021): 204–225.

Dunning, Benjamin. *Specters of Paul: Sexual Difference in Early Christian Thought*. Philadelphia, PA: University of Pennsylvania Press, 2011.

Erismann, Christophe. "A Logician for East and West: Maximus the Confessor on Universals," in *A Saint for East and West*. Daniel Haynes, ed. Eugene, OR: Cascade Books, 2019, 50–68.

Fatum, Lone. "Image of God and Glory of Man: Women in the Pauline Congregations," in *The Image of God: Gender Models in Judaeo-Christian Tradition*. Kari Børresen, ed. Minneapolis, MN: Fortress Press, 1995, 56–137.

Garrigues, Juan-Miguel. *Maxime le Confesseur: La charité, avenir divin de l'homme.* Paris: Éditions Beauchesne, 1976.

Gold, Barbara. "'And I Became a Man': Gender Fluidity and Closure in Perpetua's Passion Narrative," in *Roman Literature, Gender, and Reception.* Donald Lateiner, Barbara K. Gold, and Judith Perkins, eds. New York: Routledge, 2013, 153–165.

Green, Monica. "Bodily Essences," in *A Cultural History of the Human Body in the Middle Ages.* Linda Kalof, ed. New York: Berg, 2010, 149–171, 264–268.

Heiberg, J., ed. *Paulus Aegineta, 2 vols.* Leipzig: Teubner, 1921, 1924.

Holmes, Brooke. *Gender: Antiquity, and Its Legacy.* Oxford: Oxford University Press, 2012.

Ilberg, Johannes, ed. *Sorani Gynaeciorum libri iv, de signis fracturarum, de fasciis, vita Hippocratis secundum Soranum.* Leipzig: Teubner, 1927.

Kaldellis, Anthony. *The New Roman Empire: A History of Byzantium.* Oxford: Oxford University Press, 2024.

Khitruk, Ekaterina Borisovna. "Концептуализация отношения пола к устроению человека в патристической традиции II–VII вв.," *Vyestnik Tomskogo Gosudarstvenogo Universityeta* 365 (2012): 45–50.

King, Helen. *The One-Sex Body on Trial: The Classical and Early Modern Evidence.* New York: Routledge, 2016.

Kochańczyk-Bonińska, Karolina. "Maximus' Concept of the Sexes: The Reason and Purposes of the Distinction Between Man and Woman," *Maximus the Confessor as a European Philosopher.* Sotiris Mitralexis, Georgios Steiris, Marcin Pobdielski, and Sebastian Lalla, eds. Eugene, OR: Cascade, 2017, 229–237.

Kuefler, Mathew. *The Manly Eunuch: Masculinity, Gender Ambiguity, and Christian Ideology in Late Antiquity.* Chicago, IL: University of Chicago Press, 2001.

Kühn, Carl., ed. *Claudii Galeni opera omnia* 4. Leipzig: Knobloch, 1822.

Lake, Kirsopp and John Oulton, eds. and trans. *The Ecclesiastical History.* Cambridge, MA: Harvard University Press, 1953.

Laqueur, Thomas. *Making Sex: Body and Gender from the Greeks to Freud.* Cambridge, MA: Harvard University Press, 1990.

Larchet, Jean-Claude. *La divinisation de l'homme selon saint Maxime le Confesseur.* Paris: Cerf, 1996.

"La conception maximienne des énergies divines et des logoi et la théorie platonicienne des Idées," *Philotheos: International Journal of Philosophy and Theology* 4 (2004): 276–284.

Lipsett, Diane. *Desiring Conversion: Hermas, Thecla, Aseneth.* Oxford: Oxford University Press, 2010.

Littré, Émile, ed. *completes d'Hippocrate* 7. Paris: Baillière, 1851.

Louth, Andrew. *Maximus the Confessor.* London: Routledge, 1996.

Ludlow, Morwenna. *Universal Salvation: Eschatology in the Thought of Gregory of Nyssa and Karl Rahner.* Oxford: Oxford University Press, 2000.

MacDonald, Dennis Ronald. *There Is No Male and Female: The Fate of a Dominical Saying in Paul and Gnosticism.* Minneapolis, MN: Fortress Press, 1987.

Marcos, Natalio Fernández and Angel Sáenz-Badillos, eds. *Theodoreti quaestiones in Octateuchum.* Madrid: Poliglota Matritense, 1979.

Martin, Dale. *Sex and the Single Savior: Gender and Sexuality in Biblical Interpretation.* Louisville, KY: Westminster John Knox Press, 2006.

Marunová, Magdalena. "Nourishment in Paradise and After Resurrection: Double Creation According to Gregory of Nyssa," *Perichoresis* 19.4 (2021): 55–63.

McGowenn Tress, Daryl. "The Metaphysical Science of Aristotle's *Generation of Animals* and Its Feminist Critics," in *Feminism and Ancient Philosophy*, Julie K. Ward, ed. New York: Routledge, 1996, 31–50.

Meeks, Wayne. "The Image of the Androgyne: Some Uses of a Symbol in Earliest Christianity," *History of Religions* 13.3 (1974): 165–208.

Milkov, Kostake. "Maximus and the Healing of the Sexual Division of Creation," *Knowing the Purpose of Creation Through the Resurrection: Proceedings of the Symposium on St. Maximus the Confessor.* Bishop Maxim Vasiljević, ed. Alhambra, CA: Sebastian Press, 2013, 427–436.

Mira, Manuel. "El doblete ΛΟΓΟΣ- ΤΡΟΠΟΣ en la antropología de Máximo el Confesor," *Studia Ephemeridis Augustinianum* 140 (2014): 685–696.

Mitralexis, Sotiris. "Maximus' 'Logical' Ontology: An Introduction and Interpretative Approach to Maximus the Confessor's Notion of the *λόγοι*," *Sobornost* 37.1 (2015): 65–82.

    "Rethinking the Problem of Sexual Difference in *Ambiguum* 41," *Analogia* 2 (2017): 139–144.

    "An Attempt at Clarifying Maximus the Confessor's Remarks on (the Fate of) Sexual Difference in *Ambiguum* 41," *Philosophy and Society* 32.2 (2021): 194–203.

Neville, Leonora. *Byzantine Gender.* Leeds: Arc Humanities Press, 2019.

Nifosi, Ada. *Becoming a Woman and Mother in Greco-Roman Egypt: Women's Bodies, Society, and Domestic Space.* London: Routledge, 2019.

Odorico, P. "La cultura della ΣΥΛΛΟΓΗ," *Byzantinische Zeitschrift* 83.1 (1990): 1–21.

Olivieri, Alexander., ed. *Aëtii Amideni libri medicinales i–iv*. Leipzig: Teubner, 1935.

Olivieri, Alexander., ed. *Aëtii Amideni libri medicinales v–viii*. Berlin: Akademie-Verlag, 1950.

Ohme, Heinz. *Kirche in der Krise: Zum Streit um die Christologie im 7. Jahrhundert*. Berlin: De Gruyter, 2022.

Partridge, Cameron. "Transfiguring Sexual Difference in Maximus the Confessor," PhD Dissertation, Cambridge, MA: Harvard University, 2008.

Paul Bedjan, ed. *Acta martyrum et sanctorum* 5. Paris: Harrassowitz Verlag, 1890.

Peck, Arthur., trans. and ed. *Generation of Animals*. Cambridge, MA: Harvard University Press, 1943.

Penn, Michael. *Envisioning Islam: Syriac Christians and the Early Muslim World*. Philadelphia, PA: University of Pennsylvania Press, 2015.

Purpura, Ashley. *God, Hierarchy, Power: Orthodox Theologies of Authority from Byzantium*. New York: Fordham University Press, 2017.

Puschmann, Theodor., ed. *Alexander von Tralles, vols. 1–2*. Vienna: Braumüller, 1879.

Ringrose, Kathryn. *The Perfect Servant: Eunuchs and the Social Construction of Gender in Byzantium*. Chicago, IL: University of Chicago Press, 2007.

"The Byzantine Body," in *The Oxford Handbook of Women and Gender in Medieval Europe*. Judith Bennett and Ruth Karras, eds. Oxford: Oxford University Press, 2013, 362–378.

Rackham, Harris., ed. and trans. *Aristotle: Politics*. Cambridge, MA: Harvard University Press, 1972.

Rosser, Sue. *Women, Science, and Myth: Gender and Beliefs from Antiquity to the Present*. Santa Barbara, CA: ABC-CLIO, 2008.

Salés, Luis Josué. "'Can These Bones Live?': Gregory of Nyssa's Appropriation of Aristotelian Psychology in *On the Soul and the Resurrection*," *Sacris Erudiri* 56 (2017): 33–63.

"Queerly Christified Bodies: Women Martyrs, Christification, and the Compulsory Masculinisation Thesis," *Journal of Early Christian History* 10.3 (2020): 83–109.

"The Other Life of Maximos the Confessor: A Reevaluation of the Syriac and Greek Lives and the Case for His Alexandrian Origin," *Journal of Late Antiquity* 13.2 (2020): 407–439.

"Androprimacy: A New Analytical Concept for the Study of Gender and Religion with Case Studies from the Ethiopic Didəsqəlya and the Greek Apostolic Constitutions," in *Gender and Religion* 12 (2022): 195–213.

"Maximos' Correspondence with Egyptian Women: Introduction, Critical Commentary, and Translation of *Letters* 11 and 18," *Subsidia Maximiana* 3. Vladimir Cvetković and Alexis Léonas, eds. Turnhout: Brepols (in press).

Shoemaker, Stephen. *The Death of a Prophet: The End of Muhammad's Life and the Beginnings of Islam*. Philadelphia, PA: University of Pennsylvania Press, 2012.

Sonea, Cristian-Sebastian. "Man's Mission as Mediator for the Entire World according to Saint Maximus' Confessor's Theology," *International Journal of Orthodox Theology* 3.3 (2012): 181–185.

Storti, Gemma. "Metrodora's Work on the Diseases of Women and Their Cures," *Estudios bizantinos* 6 (2018): 89–110.

Szczerba, Wojciech. "Podwójne stworzenie a soteriologia Grzegorza z Nyssy," *Poznańskie Studia Teologiczne* 22 (2008): 91–101.

Talbot, Alice-Mary, ed. *Holy Women of Byzantium*, Washington, DC: Dumbarton Oaks, 1996.

Thunberg, Lars. *Microcosm and Mediator: The Theological Anthropology of Maximus the Confessor*, 2nd ed. Chicago, IL: Open Court, 1995.

Tollefsen, Torstein. *The Christocentric Cosmology of St Maximus the Confessor*. Oxford: Oxford University Press, 2008.

Tredennick, Hugh and Cyril Armstrong, eds. and trans. *Aristotle: Metaphysics, Books 10-14. Oeconomica. Magna Moralia*. Cambridge, MA: Harvard University Press, 1935.

Vilimonović, Larisa. "Gender, Diseases, and Sexuality in the Writings of Soranus, Aetius of Amida and Paul of Aegina: Contributions to the Anthropology of Disease in Byzantium," *Etnoantropološki Problemi* 17.4 (2022): 1203–1224.

Walters, Jonathan. "Invading the Roman Body: Manliness and Impenetrability in Roman Thought," *Roman Sexualities*. Judith P. Hallett and Marilyn Skinner, eds. Princeton: Princeton University Press, 1998, 29–43.

Wilberding, James. *Forms, Souls, and Embryos: Neoplatonists on Human Reproduction*. London: Routledge, 2017.

Zachhuber, Johannes. *Human Nature in Gregory of Nyssa: Philosophical Background and Theological Significance*. Leiden: Brill, 2014.

Zervos, Skevos., ed. *Gynaekologie des Aëtios*. Leipzig: Fock, 1901.

This Element is dedicated to Orthodox Christian women everywhere, and especially to Katya, whose love and support made this project possible.

Cambridge Elements ≡

Early Christian Literature

Garrick V. Allen
University of Glasgow

Garrick V. Allen (PhD St Andrews, 2015) is Professor of Divinity and Biblical Criticism at the University of Glasgow. He is the author of multiple articles and books on the New Testament, early Jewish and Christian literature, and ancient and medieval manuscript traditions, including *Manuscripts of the Book of Revelation: New Philology, Paratexts, Reception* (Oxford University Press, 2020) and *Words are Not Enough: Paratexts, Manuscripts, and the Real New Tesatament* (Eerdmans, 2024). He is the winner of the Manfred Lautenschlaeger Award for Theological Promise and the Paul J. Achetemeier Award for New Testament Scholarship.

About the Series

This series sets new research agendas for understanding early Christian literature, exploring the diversity of Christian literary practices through the contexts of ancient literary production, the forms of literature composed by early Christians, themes related to particular authors, and the languages in which these works were written.

Cambridge Elements ≡

Early Christian Literature

Elements in the Series

Maximos the Confessor: Anaroprimacy and Sexual Difference
Luis Josué Salés

A full series listing is available at: www.cambridge.org/EECL

For EU product safety concerns, contact us at Calle de José Abascal, 56–1°,
28003 Madrid, Spain or eugpsr@cambridge.org.

www.ingramcontent.com/pod-product-compliance
Ingram Content Group UK Ltd.
Pitfield, Milton Keynes, MK11 3LW, UK
UKHW022135110325
456116UK00010B/297